Emerging Practices in Architectural Pedagogy

Emerging Practices in Architectural Pedagogy explores the emergent techniques in architectural education that are helping to bridge the gap between the institutional setting and working practice. It demonstrates how teaching and learning can, and should, be directed towards tackling the real-world problems that students will encounter within their future professional careers. Architectural and design practitioners are becoming less specialised, they are embracing cross-disciplinary connections and practical problem-solving. Architecture and design schools must align their teaching to reflect this changing world, and evolve from a fact-based acquisition process to a participatory method of learning.

This book uses an extended case-study format to examine large-scale issues. Each chapter represents a specific mode of practice, which is linked to the wider debate on architectural and design pedagogy; this includes collaborative workshops and interventions, issues connected to sustainability and climate change, responses to rapid urbanisation, and, the creation of collaborative relationships across disciplines.

The book has an international perspective, with contributions from the United Kingdom, the United States of America, and Singapore, and includes a timely discussion on teaching in a remote climate. This book will be an invaluable resource for engaged academics and teaching practitioners interested in playing a key role in the future development of the architectural profession.

Laura Sanderson's work focuses upon the process of analysing and understanding the nature and qualities of place, in order to develop new buildings and other elements within the environment of the already built. As the Atelier Leader for Continuity in Architecture, she has led funded projects in settlements around Manchester; producing research outputs from projects in Bollington (2016), Bakewell (2017), Rochdale (2019), Shrewsbury (2020), and this year in Bradford. These outputs include exhibitions, articles, interactive children's projects, book chapters, and built interventions. Laura co-curated UnDoing (2019), an exhibition at th radical independent Castlefield Gallery (with Sally Stone), featuring the work of a number of international artists and architects, exploring how buildings, places, and artefacts are re-used, reinterpreted, and remembered. These themes will be further explored in the forthcoming book "Remember, Reveal, Construct: Reflections upon the Contingency, Usefulness and Emotional Resonance of Architecture, Buildings and Context" (with Sally Stone 2022). Another imminent project is a collaboration with Luca Csepely-Knorr and the Institute of Place Management examining the High Streets of the District Centres of Manchester. Laura has published a number of reflections on her pedagogic approach including the work in Continuity in Architecture, the Atelier Zero installation, and the MSA Events Programme (with Vicky Jolley), which has produced over 200 diverse live projects over the past decade. Laura Sanderson is an Architect, a Senior Lecturer at Manchester School of Architecture, Year Leader for the Master of Architecture Programme and Atelier Leader for Continuity in Architecture.

For more than thirty years **Sally Stone** has been designing, discussing, formulating ideas, and writing about architecture, building reuse, and interiors. She recently published "UnDoing Buildings: Adaptation and Cultural Memory," and she is also the co-author of a number of other books including "ReReadings Volumes 1 & 2," "From Organisation to Decoration," and the series: "Interior Architecture: An Approach." She co-curated the exhibition "UnDoing" at the radical independent Castlefield Gallery in the centre of Manchester, which explored the disconnected yet similar approaches that artist and architects take to the already existing (interior) environment (with Laura Sanderson). "Remember Reveal Construct: Reflections upon the Contingency, Usefulness and Emotional Resonance of Architecture, Buildings and Context" (with Laura Sanderson) will be published in 2022. Sally is the co-recipient of the UK Government sponsored Heritage Heroes Award in recognition of her work to save the Preston Bus Station. Sally Stone directs the Atelier Continuity in Architecture, and leads the Master of Architecture and the MA Architecture and Adaptive Reuse programme at the Manchester School of Architecture.

Routledge Focus on Design Pedagogy
Series Editor: Graham Cairns

The Routledge Focus on Design Pedagogy series provides the reader with the latest scholarship for instructors who educate designers. The series publishes research from across the globe and covers areas as diverse as beginning design and foundational design, architecture, product design, interior design, fashion design, landscape architecture, urban design, and architectural conservation and historic preservation. By making these studies available to the worldwide academic community, the series aims to promote quality design education.

Fluid Space and Transformational Learning
Kyriaki Tsoukala

Progressive Studio Pedagogy
Examples from Architecture and Allied Design Fields
Edited by Charlie Smith

Emerging Practices in Architectural Pedagogy
Accommodating an Uncertain Future
Edited by Laura Sanderson and Sally Stone

For more information about this series, please visit: https://www.routledge.com/architecture/series/RFDP

Emerging Practices in Architectural Pedagogy
Accommodating an Uncertain Future

Edited by Laura Sanderson and Sally Stone

LONDON AND NEW YORK

First published 2022
by Routledge
2 Park Square, Milton Park, Abingdon, Oxon OX14 4RN

and by Routledge
605 Third Avenue, New York, NY 10158

Routledge is an imprint of the Taylor & Francis Group, an informa business

© 2022 selection and editorial matter, Laura Sanderson and Sally Stone; individual chapters, the contributors

The right of Laura Sanderson and Sally Stone to be identified as the authors of the editorial material, and of the authors for their individual chapters, has been asserted in accordance with sections 77 and 78 of the Copyright, Designs and Patents Act 1988.

All rights reserved. No part of this book may be reprinted or reproduced or utilised in any form or by any electronic, mechanical, or other means, now known or hereafter invented, including photocopying and recording, or in any information storage or retrieval system, without permission in writing from the publishers.

Trademark notice: Product or corporate names may be trademarks or registered trademarks, and are used only for identification and explanation without intent to infringe.

British Library Cataloguing-in-Publication Data
A catalogue record for this book is available from the British Library

Library of Congress Cataloging-in-Publication Data
Names: Sanderson, Laura, editor. | Stone, Sally, editor.
Title: Emerging practices in architectural pedagogy : accommodating an uncertain future / edited by Laura Sanderson and Sally Stone.
Description: Abingdon, Oxon ; New York : Routledge, 2022. | Series: Routledge focus on design pedagogy | Includes bibliographical references and index.
Identifiers: LCCN 2021015429 (print) | LCCN 2021015430 (ebook) | ISBN 9781032004150 (hardback) | ISBN 9781032004204 (paperback) | ISBN 9781003174080 (ebook)
Subjects: LCSH: Architecture--Study and teaching.
Classification: LCC NA2000 .E44 2021 (print) | LCC NA2000 (ebook) | DDC 720.71--dc23
LC record available at https://lccn.loc.gov/2021015429
LC ebook record available at https://lccn.loc.gov/2021015430

ISBN: 9781032004150 (hbk)
ISBN: 9781032004204 (pbk)
ISBN: 9781003174080 (ebk)

DOI: 10.4324/9781003174080

Typeset in Times
by KnowledgeWorks Global Ltd.

Contents

List of contributors viii
Foreword xii

Introduction 1
SALLY STONE AND LAURA SANDERSON

1 **Pedagogy + workshop: Public CoLab 2019: Tracing Belfast's water** 16
NUALA FLOOD AND TRISTAN STURM

2 **Pedagogy + exhibition: _mpathic design** 36
ELGIN CLECKLEY

3 **Pedagogy + intervention: Cumulus, an inhabitable storm** 53
MILAGROS ZINGONI AND MAGNUS FEIL

4 **Pedagogy + production space: Steam & the city** 73
ALESSANDRO COLUMBANO

5 **Pedagogy + policy: Rochdale reimagined** 94
SALLY STONE AND LAURA SANDERSON

6 **Pedagogy + resilience: Designing resilience in Asia International Research Program** 116
OSCAR CARRACEDO GARCÍA-VILLALBA

Index 137

List of contributors

Oscar Carracedo García-Villalba is an architect, urban designer, planner, and educator, currently Assistant Professor at the Department of Architecture, National University of Singapore. He is the director of the Master of Urban Design at NUS, director of the DRIA-Designing Resilience in Asia International Research Program, director and research leader of the ETH-Future Cities Global-Sea/City Cluster, and principal leader of the Singapore Center for Urban Resilience (SeCURE) where he develops his research on urbanisation processes, climate change, urban resilience, sustainability, regenerative urbanism, decarbonised futures, and integrated urban planning. Oscar is the author of numerous books and articles, and drawing on his rigorous research, he has recently published "Designing Resilience in Asia. Planning the unpredictable, designing with uncertainty" (ACTAR, 2021), "Resilient Urban Regeneration in Informal Settlements in the Tropics" (Springer, 2020), "Silicon Singapore. Urban Projects for Hybrid and Resilient Innovation Districts" (Basheer, 2020), "Ibid./ In the same place. Nine Lessons and Six Possibilities about On-site Resilient Revitalization Strategies for Informal Neighbourhoods" (ORO, 2016), "Indus_hoods. From industries to Neighbourhoods" (CASA-JTC-i3, 2016), and the co-edited volume "Advanced Studies in Energy Efficiency and Built Environment for Developing Countries" (Springer, 2019). Oscar has been invited to present as a keynote speaker in 16 countries in five continents, and is actively engaged as an expert with UN-Habitat, The World Bank Group, World Resources Institute, GRCN, C40, and many other reputable international institutions. Oscar is also the CEO and co-founder of CSArchitects slp, an urban planning, urban design, and architecture firm based in Barcelona, Spain, and Singapore. Oscar has won two national urban planning and design prizes. His work and research has been awarded in more than 40 national and international competitions and has been published nationally and internationally.

Elgin Cleckley, NOMA, is an Assistant Professor of Architecture at the University of Virginia School of Architecture with an appointment in the Curry School of Education and the School of Nursing. He is a designer and principal of _mpathic design – a Design Thinking pedagogy, initiative, and professional practice focusing on identity, culture, history, memory, and place. After studying architecture at the University of Virginia and Princeton University, Elgin collaborated with DLR Group (Seattle), MRSA Architects (Chicago), and Baird Sampson Neuert Architects (Toronto) on award-winning civic projects. Before joining UVA's Design Thinking program in 2016, he was the 3D Group Leader and Design Coordinator at the Ontario Science Centre (Toronto), Science Content and Design Department, and Agents of Change Initiative. This work produced the world's first museum/design thinking architecture space (the Weston Family Innovation Centre), featuring award-winning exhibitions, educational facilities, and public art with international artists. _mpathic design's practice includes national and local collaborations. Elgin is also the Design Director at the UVA Equity Center.

Alessandro Columbano is a Senior Lecturer at the Birmingham School of Architecture and Design. His academic roles include MArch (RIBA Pt.2) Course Director and School Lead for Enterprise & Innovation. Alessandro co-established and leads the Co\\aborative Lab:oratory (Co.LAB) a design & research initiative within the school that integrates teaching with interdisciplinary creative practice through live projects, staff research, and design consultancy. Co.LAB has been part of over 100 collaborative projects, with over 50 partners spanning community groups, arts organisations, civic institutions, and industrial partners. It has designed a number of creative spaces in the city including Birmingham Open Media, Centrala Gallery, and The Dual Works workshop, developing a unique insight into the creative industry and artistic community in Birmingham. In 2014, Alessandro was co-investigator for the Birmingham Production Space, a proposal for a centre of production for artists which was a precursor to STEAMhouse, a prototyping and innovation centre for the West Midlands. Alessandro brings this knowledge and expertise to his teaching as an academic and researcher; taking an active role in the discussion of architectural pedagogy, urban regeneration and contemporary workplaces. It is applied by engaging the city's cultural network and supporting students in entrepreneurial activity as part of their curriculum, championing organisations with civic causes, and fostering a community of makers, designers, and active citizens.

Assistant Professor **Magnus Feil** received his MFA in Industrial Design from The Ohio State University and a Diplom (FH) from Fachhochschule für Gestaltung, Schwäbisch Gmünd, Germany. He came to the United States as a Fulbright scholar in 2000. His research interests are product design in aviation and medicine; product interaction: control of views, vehicles, and robotic platforms, and aspects that guide form in industrial and interaction design. Magnus has received the Red Dot Award for Excellence in Design by the Designzentrum Nordrhein-Westfalen, Germany in 2002 and the iF product design award of the International Forum Design Hannover, Germany in 2003. Magnus worked as a product designer for B/S/H GmbH in Munich, Germany, as a design consultant for Siemens Corporate Research Inc. in Princeton, New Jersey, and as HMI design consultant for Johnson Controls Inc., in Burscheid, Germany. Before joining ASU's Herberger Institute for Design and the Arts, Magnus held a faculty position at the University of Washington in Seattle, WA.

Nuala Flood is a Senior Lecturer in Architecture at Queen's University Belfast (QUB) where she is also the director of the BSc Architecture Programme. Her transdisciplinary research explores how codesign methods, ecotopian design fictions, urban interventionist practices, and participatory mapping can be used to contextualise socio-spatial and environmental issues. Her work with Dr Tristan Sturm (QUB Human Geography) traces the multidimensional place-based consequences of lead contamination of the water system in Belfast. In 2017 she created the award-winning pedagogical experience, Public CoLab, where teams of architecture students work with external partners and subject experts to investigate the place-based manifestations of wicked phenomena such as climate change adaptation, the compromised water system and, most recently, the COVID-proofed city. Her research has been published widely in academic journals and international conferences, and has also been disseminated via exhibitions, installations, and workshops. As an ARB registered architect, she has designed and managed the construction of large-scale energy-efficient office developments, social housing projects, and public library schemes.

Tristan Sturm is Senior Lecturer in Geography at Queen's University Belfast. He is interested in public health geographies, specifically lead pipe infrastructure and lead exposure (on which he works closely with the architecture scholar, Nuala Flood), and apocalyptic thought related to climate change, conspiracies, and religious movements in the United States of America and Israel/Palestine. Recently he has been researching how COVID-19 conspiracies borrow from Christian apocalyptic thought. His recent paper in Anthropology & Medicine (written with Tom Albrecht) argues that as the semiotics and motivations for COVID apocalyptic conspiratorial thinking are more or less the same across the left and right political spectrum, there is an opening for contestatory apocalyptic politics to destabilise coronavirus capitalism and cultivate constituencies for change across evangelical, leftward, and rightward positionalities toward Žižek's "impossible political alliance." He has published over 25 academic articles/chapters and has disseminated his findings in the Toronto Star, Haaretz, Jerusalem Post, National Post, THE Magazine, Journal.ie, BBC radio 4, among other media spaces. He is currently finishing a book entitled, *The Future is a Foreign Country: Christian Zionists and Landscapes of the Apocalypse in Israel/Palestine*. He is co-editor with Jason Dittmer of Mapping the End Times (also with Routledge).

Associate Professor **Milagros Zingoni** is the Director of the School of Interior Architecture at the University of Tennessee Knoxville. She began teaching architecture and urban design as an adjunct faculty in 2005 before joining the interior design and interior architecture programs in 2013. Zingoni is originally from Argentina, where she is a registered architect, and has additional study Habitat Design (Bachelor)) and Urban and Environmental Planning (Master). Milagros's experience as both a designer and educator provides a fresh lens to understand student-centred approaches both physically and pedagogically. Her research includes explorations of environmental and experiential settings that address new ways of learning and how these settings emphasise problem-solving skills and collaboration that creates communities of learning. Her studios focus on community and commitment to public engagement through participatory design-build collaboration. Zingoni was recognised in 2019 by the Interior Design Educator's Council (IDEC) with the National Teaching Excellence Award, by the American Institute of Architects (AIA) Arizona Chapter with the honour of 2019 Educators of the Year Award, by the annual Design Intelligence rankings as one of the top twelve most admired educators in the country and by Arizona State University 2020 Outstanding Faculty Mentor Awards. Zingoni is a strong advocate for community causes, serving on multiple non-profit and civic boards.

Foreword

Graham Cairns

Pedagogy and practice in flux: Comments on design

It is, in 2021, stating the obvious to say that the Coronavirus pandemic has fundamentally changed the way educators operate. It is equally obvious to identify that the changes to modes of operation in professional contexts have changed in an equally radical manner. Whether it be our working methods as individuals or in teams; the ways in which we interact with clients globally; the increased use of digital technologies in the conceptualisation, design and presentation of projects; or in the requirements set of the projects we are now engaged with, "change" is seemingly omniscient. The inevitable flux that the design professions and their educational counterparts have already experienced, and will be witnesses to moving forward, means that how we operate as educators and designers in the coming years will, in many ways, be unrecognisable.

However, it is also important to remember that the pandemic is only one of the forces pushing design education and practice in new directions, albeit one whose impact was almost instantaneous. As this book illustrates, and at times explicitly underlines, many of the issues we grapple with as designers and design educators can be considered to "transcend" the questions of a changed working environment and professional landscape. Indeed, they existed before the pandemic, were operative throughout it, and will remain of the utmost importance thereafter. This book thus hints at the diffuseness and complexity of the future in sometimes surprising ways and, as such, makes an excellent contribution to the *Routledge Focus on Design Pedagogy* series of which it forms a part.

The series shares many of the concerns laid out by the editors of this volume with regard to changing nature of the design and the education sector. Indeed, the very establishment of the series is an attempt to acknowledge this and provide a platform through which educators and designers can contribute to the diverse debates around it. As one of the early issues in the series, this volume is a highly valuable publication for those seeking to better understand the emerging nature of design education and specifically, in my view, three sets of issues the editors have drawn out and which I will reiterate by way of overview.

Firstly, the chapters in this book all respond in their own particular ways to what the editors have defined as "an expanded definition" of architectural and design practice and, by extension, an expanded definition of what design education needs to be. That expanded definition of the architect and the designer is, in the specific case of architecture, reflected in the challenges to the term "architect" itself and its protected status within the United Kingdom and further afield. This challenge reflects the reality of a profession that now functions in very different ways. It is a profession that has moved away from a reading of the designer of a building as being a form of master craftsman. What now predominates is a definition that sees the role of the designer as a facilitator and coordinator of multiple efforts from fellow professionals, as well as a full range of stakeholders impacted by, and involved in, the design of the built environment.

The second issue I feel the editors encapsulate in their introduction is a recognition of design as being inextricably embedded in a broader professional and societal context. It is an issue reflected in the increased propensity in design education to engage in collaborations with players we define as operating in the "real world," often formulated in the Academy through the term problem-based learning. A corollary of this is a view of design as engaged in "Wicked Problems" beyond the reach of any individual or professional knowledge base. It shifts attention in education from knowledge acquisition to the development of skills that allow for the sourcing, interpretation, and use of knowledge on a "need to know" or "need to use" basis. In fields such as fashion design and other retail sectors, this finds an echo in the idea of "just in time delivery": a process in which the whole design, manufacture, and delivery of products responds to unpredictable and unknown opportunities and problems on a constantly changing basis, often at short notice, and using techniques not necessarily pre-existent. The problem-based learning approach then is a methodology that demands from the students a greater understanding, plus the ability to work across disciplines and stakeholder groups, and also accentuates the need to embrace a collaborative approach to knowledge and conventional disciplinary expertise to create something that is unrecognisable to that which dominated only a generation ago.

Issues such as this clearly not only affect the practice of design but also, as again the editors of this volume underline very succinctly, modes of teaching. To remain relevant for students whose professions are in flux, and whose futures will be marked by unpredictability, our forms of pedagogy need to evolve. We need to facilitate a student's ability to take on the yet to be imagined projects of the future, as well as the complex reality of those already on the table. A continual evolution and experimentation in how we operate as educators are thus also central to this book and represent the third big picture theme I see running through its pages.

In focusing on this issue the editors and the contributing authors to this volume introduce a number of innovative models for education that include, amongst many others: the incorporation of "empathy" into the recognised toolkit of designers; the development of expressly interdisciplinary collaborations for students in which their need to share knowledge and responsibility across sectors is paramount; the engagement of students with real-world problems such as city resilience and/or real-world players such as community "clients" or government authorities. It all involves not only imagination in the setting of projects but rigour and insight in the analysis of relevant pedagogy – found in this book through educational and communicative concepts and models such EDIT (engagement, design, implementation, transformation) and E.M.P.A.T.H.Y. (Eye contact; Muscles of facial expression; Posture; Affect; Tone of voice; Hearing the whole patient; Your response).

The editors of this volume have done an excellent job in the introduction to contextualise such issues as they manifest themselves in contemporary pedagogical literature and in the work of the book's authors specifically. As such, I do not need to comment on individual chapters here. It is suffice to say that arguments that readers will find in this volume are all thought-provoking and insightful and, I expect, will be highly useful for any design educator. They will be particularly useful to those in the spatial design fields with an interest in the three issues highlighted here: the expanded definition of design, the increased importance of problem-based learning in design, and emerging modes of pedagogy that respond to this.

Introduction

Sally Stone and Laura Sanderson

Introduction

Over the last generation, the position of the architect and designer has radically changed. In the face of increased complexity, rapidly advancing digital practices, evolving expectations, the climate emergency, the need for densification, and the necessity for diversification, the architect/designer is facing an uncertain future. A future in which the expectations placed upon them has evolved far from the formal and traditional professional status of the last century. Different opportunities combined with interconnected critical issues, and, the fluctuating status of the profession means that the role of the architect, just like many other professionals, is being challenged. So, the architect in the 21st century is expected to lead less and facilitate more. They are vitally important members of a complex team, all of whom have an important role to play within the development of the built environment.

Architectural and design education has to evolve to reflect this change. The manner in which students are being taught needs to understand how and why these revisions have occurred and how to accommodate this new future. The majority of today's students will, by 2030, be working in jobs that haven't yet been invented, and schools of architecture and design need to be implementing policies that reflect this new world.[1] This doesn't mean that professions like architecture will become obsolete, but their contribution and their role will be different; overlapping and involving collaboration with many more subject areas.

All educational practices are transforming. Digitisation and the internet mean that all information is now easily accessible, the average smartphone can access as much material as any National Library holds. So, the problem is not the acquisition of knowledge but the contextualisation of this intelligence. How, in a world of excess information, can this information be understood? In an age of infinitely expanding and circulating intelligence, when dictionaries and encyclopaedia are obsolete almost before they are even printed, how can any student understand the acquired information, how can they contextualise this and then and most importantly, how can they make use of it?

Thus architectural education, like its related fields, is rapidly developing; from a fact-based acquisition process to a participatory method of learning. It is not sufficient to expect a student to design a complex building on a clean site with unknown users. All educational practices are beginning to use methods of learning where knowledge is acquired on a need-to-know basis rather than using a universal approach of instilling particular facts into the student. But the facilitation of this need-to-know process has a difficult and somewhat hazy methodology. How, in the rapidly evolving arena of architectural education, can this approach be formulated? The necessity to reflect the approach of the professional is implicit within all architectural and design education. Architect and educator, Nick Hayhurst, discussing an unpublished lecture by the architectural professional theorist, Rory Hyde, explained that he believed that what was wrong with the profession is its narrow focus on design and the belief that the building is the project, stating that "the project is the client: perhaps society, perhaps future users, perhaps the environment … but the project certainly isn't the building."[2]

Architecture is a unique discipline that is widely connected to other subjects. Therefore the future of architectural education can be examined through the prism of several directly related disciplines, including urban planning, spatial design, interior architecture, exhibition design, construction and environmental engineering, and, of course, architecture itself. Schools and faculties need to be implementing policies that promote teaching excellence, that encourage a student-centred curriculum, that support international dialogue and collaboration (especially in this time of uncertainty), and create global citizens.

There are many challenges that are directly facing education, including COVID-19, the need for diversity, austerity, and the impact of the digital revolution. Students must leave education with skill sets that equip them for life in a changing and evolving landscape of possibilities. They must be able to take advantage of the upcoming challenges and the current climate of exciting possibilities. Abigail Patel, the 2020 RIBA National Council Student Representative, described her own ambitions: "architectural education teaches us that there are no right or wrong answers but provides us with the tools and knowledge to make those informed decisions correctly."[3]

Laboratories for exploration

The position of a school of architecture and design is to provide a workshop as well as a studio in which to extrapolate futures. The next generation of graduates need to be astute, have a strong moral compass and be agile in digital networks. They will be reinventing their "profession," and if they are to participate in this process, all schools have to be further developed to create environments where all positions are possible; laboratories for exploration that provide an open field for theoretical and technical positions but applied to specific purposes. Architectural and design education is the search for radical solutions to an ever-changing world, and also importantly to the pursuit of beauty within architecture itself.

The focus of architectural and design education is becoming more diverse and the value and importance of collaboration, both for learning and personal development, is inevitable. Students are increasingly keen to engage directly with issues of social and environmental concern and connect with the world beyond the somewhat artificial atmosphere of the university. Difficult, incomplete, and contradictory problems can be addressed within the architectural programme; these "Wicked Problems" contain economic, environmental, and political issues, and need a great number of people to change their mind-set and behaviour, so at least in part can provide stimulating vehicles for exploration. Subjects included within the overriding category are those connected with climate change and environmental degradation, social responsibility, diversity, and changing priorities within domestic organisation, heritage, and the future of the already built, urban design, new materials and new methods of construction, plus health and mental wellbeing.

Architectural and design education is a laboratory for exploration and experimentation; indeed, it is the responsibility of all students of architecture to question the validity of the built environment that surrounds them. Students must be enquiring, activist, and vigilant. They should expect higher education to provide them with the means to think seriously about the world, to question the manner in which it is occupied, to look beyond the current situation, to understand why and how that has arisen and to imagine alternative futures. The next generation of architects need to be able to think laterally, to react quickly to the changing situation and at the beginning of the third decade of the 21st century to have the confidence to think beyond the expected and into a radically new future. And it is the role of the education to provide a platform for this to happen.

The introduction to the highly important "Spatial Design Education: New Directions for Pedagogy in Architecture and Beyond" by Ashraf M. Salama contains a fine survey of the major and most relevant texts on architectural education and design pedagogy, as well as a chronological description of the evolution of the subject. His narrative includes a discussion of the emergence of alternative forms of design studio teaching models that developed in the 1960s and 1970s, which explored the potential to open-up architectural pedagogy to a wider range of influences. This formed the basis of educational practices which were much more experimental, but have today become recognised pedagogical practice such as experiential learning, critical enquiry, process-based learning, community-based design learning, design-build, and live-build. However, he laments that these "emerging paradigms of design education are being expressed in contexts where academia still distances itself from the real world, still barricades itself from real human problems, and thus misses valuable opportunities to learn from the richness, depth and variety of human experience."[4]

Participatory learning

Architectural education is changing. There are emerging techniques for bridging the gap between education and the real world, whether that be the global issues of our day or how individual users engage with and benefit from design. All built environments are products of the culture that created that environment, and it is the role of the student to interrogate this, to examine and analyse the existing conditions, to upset the status quo, and to propose a different solution. Many design studio teaching practices are already global in nature; certainly, international precedents and theorists are examined within all schools worldwide.

This development in architectural and design education is highlighted by the fact that many of the projects within academia are no longer grounded in fact-based acquisition but instead use a participatory method of learning. Problem-based learning encourages the student to intimately examine a question. Instead of just learning of the problem and being informed of how to solve it, the student is encouraged to become immersed within it. This "research-through-doing" methodology requires the student to develop an insightful relationship with all of the actors within the project. This comprehensive understanding of the needs and values of all the participants (real, imaginary, built, digital, virtual) encourages a coming together of theory and design in a more fruitful way than mere examining can. Key to the approach of this book is an examination of the applicability of the architectural and design skills taught in architecture and design schools to a number of real-world scenarios. Within this discourse, it is recognised that the design studio is the principal pillar of architectural education. It is the environment in which creative exploration is conducted, interaction is encouraged, and provides a context for the acquisition of knowledge, the assimilation of this through the design process, and reflection upon this gained insight. Salama describes the design studio as the "backbone of architectural education," as a rich field of theoretical and practical discourse. However, he considers that "current processes, theories, content, methods, and tools need to be questioned and critically examined."[5] This, he argues, is because most design studios do not encourage a holistic approach to architectural education. He then lists the possible opportunities that are missed out on, such as an "awareness of socio-cultural and environmental issues, collaboration and teamwork, dialogic learning, sensitivity to and awareness of difference, critical discourse, innovative design and technical competence."[6]

Architects and designers have certain skills; they understand the built environment, they can read its character, comprehend its grain, and appreciate the inconsistencies. They also have the ability to envisage alternative futures and this ability allows them to suggest different solutions to the ones currently being pursued. Architecture and design is formed in the imagination, and architecture and design students are at the cutting edge of effective techniques to develop and visualise distinct potentials. The pedagogies uncovered in this book show how these projects sit on the boundary between academia and practice, thus enabling the development and depiction of ideas by the students that maybe professionals would not be in a position to realise.

Architectural education and real-world problems

Real-world problems take the process and product of education beyond the idea of learning as an end in itself. The development of student-designed projects can have impact that exceeds the design studio. Relationships with professionals, interested parties, and collaborators allow the students to appreciate the impact of their work and the responsibility entailed within it. Students need to be in a position to understand the complex interactive relationships that exist within the real world, but also explore ideas for the development of it from within the safety of the academic studio. The point is not to create "profession-ready" graduates, but to encourage the student to develop an inquiring approach that will sustain them throughout their professional careers. Students have opportunities that professionals do not necessarily have; maybe they can be more outrageous, more extreme, or even be in a position to develop ideas that the professional, with their exact brief and tight constraints, may not be in a position to act out.

Importantly these real projects in education do not necessarily fit into the mould of "live" projects, defined by Jane Anderson and Colin Priest as having six common factors: "external collaborator, educational organisation, brief, timescale, budget and product."[7] Many of the projects in this book are not a case of academia replicating the profession, or even undermining it by completing work for very little cost. The work that the student's complete is not necessarily viable, but it is stimulating, thought provoking, theoretically challenging, and most of all asks the right questions. It encourages the collaborators to question their own position within the built environment and empowers them to make the right decisions about its development. Students need to be aware of the constraints and possibilities within the world if they are to tackle tomorrow's "Wicked Problems." From collaborative workshops and interventions, to issues connected with sustainability and climate change, from design as a mode of participation, to responses to rapid urbanisation, new approaches to planning policy, and creating relationships with crucial partners across disciplines, these emergent projects allow the student to project and develop their own agenda and response.

These cross-disciplinary/inter-disciplinary approaches also create an environment where scholars from other cultural backgrounds and contexts, and from different disciplinary interests can learn from each other, creating a dynamic and productive environment for effective learning. Working with outside agencies provides a useful seed bed for various organisations to be familiar with the students' activities, their level of knowledge, and consequently lead them to provide further input to the discipline. Teaching and learning practices can, and maybe should, be directed towards tackling tomorrow's "Wicked Problems" in ways that can challenge the future of architectural and related design education itself.

Accommodating an uncertain future

It is the Spring of 2021, and we are in the middle of the COVID-19 pandemic. All architecture and design educators are grappling with changes in the landscape of the profession; the dramatic move to online learning, the necessity to interact across wide distances, the imperative to keep students engaged with particular places that they may not have visited and are possibly completely alien to them, and the need to do this with unfailing fortitude and optimism.

Writing the chapters of this book coincided exactly within the period of the pandemic, in a state of change; a time of enforced lockdown, restricted movement, and limited physical interaction. They began as a series of papers presented at the "Education, Design and Practice – Understanding skills in a Complex World" conference hosted by AMPS (Architecture, Media, Politics, Society) in collaboration with the Stevens Institute of Technology which took place New Jersey, USA in 2019. The conference was the summer before the first case of COVID-19 was reported, in what seems now like a different world – an extraordinary time where physical interaction was possible and simple social actions, such as drinking a cup of coffee in a café with a colleague were normal. Inevitably the pandemic has had a massive affect upon the education of architects and designers and many of the chapters reflect upon this.

The conference itself highlighted innovative approaches to teaching architecture and design, and foregrounded collaborative and cross-disciplinary practice. The initial call for papers discussed the complex relationship between education and practice, stating that, "today, educators in the liberal arts still identify learning as an end unto itself, and designers still draw on ideas about intuitive knowledge. By contrast, the businesses behind urban development or city and regional growth call for graduates armed with the skills required in practice from day one. At the same time local government and cultural or city management firms need creative thinkers capable of continual adaptation. In the industries and sectors such as construction, transport and engineering, managers focus on a foundational baseline, and value engineers and designers as both pragmatic problem solvers and visionaries."[8]

There is not really the time nor the distance to reflect upon the great adjustments to education that will be wrought by the pandemic, but it is sufficient to acknowledge that things will not go back to the way they were. It was evident that digital practices were already instigating change, making international collaboration more possible, invitations to visitors and critics easier, and encouraging immediate worldwide connections. But this evolution may have taken 30 years rather than 30 days. Let us hope that we retain the good stuff and realise what doesn't or shouldn't work.

Another recent event of climactic consequence was the death of George Floyd and the consequent rise in the Black Lives Matter campaign. This appalling incident has encouraged educators to look at the manner in which they impart information, the resources they use, the architects and designers they quote from, and the designers that they encourage their students to learn from. Alleviating unconscious bias is not just about social stereotypes, but also means ensuring that all available people and cultures are represented. The influence of groups who may have been underrepresented in the design industry is actively sought, and this conscious assimilation of all cultures will certainly widen the power and authority of the architecture and design industry, but also make it fit for everyone.

Chapter introductions

Taking an international perspective, the papers selected for this book were chosen for both their similarities and their differences. They are similar in their approach (all are collaborative responses to "Wicked Problems") and in their voice (all are primary accounts written by the academics directly involved). They differ however in the theme they are exploring (from sustainability and climate change, to developing empathic design skills, to responses to rapid urbanisation) and in the mode of the final output (from workshops, to installations, to policy).

So, in the strange locked down summer of 2020, and as most universities made plans for a socially distanced curriculum, the authors expanded their papers into longer case studies; Pedagogy + Workshop (Chapter 1), Pedagogy + Exhibition (Chapter 2), Pedagogy + Intervention (Chapter 3), Pedagogy + Production Space (Chapter 4), Pedagogy + Policy (Chapter 5), and finally Pedagogy + Resilience (Chapter 6). Each chapter documents the primary experience of a pre-pandemic case study, expanded during a moment of seismic change – to which architectural and design education needs to respond, but in ways not yet completely certain.

In Chapter 1 *Pedagogy + Workshop*, Nuala Flood and Tristan Sturm discuss their project, "Public CoLab 2019: Tracing Belfast's Water," which took the form of a five-day long collaborative workshop with architecture students from Queen's University Belfast in Northern Ireland working alongside subject experts from academia (oral historians, film makers, GIS specialists, water scarcity researchers, and climate change visualisers), the public sector, and charitable organisations. The project used actor-network theory (ANT) to examine the often overlooked "actor" of water in the city of Belfast, and produced a collective zine to communicate findings to a general public audience. Embedded within the chapter is an argument that the relationship

Figure 1 Sample spread from "Flooding Futures" in *Tracing Belfast's Water*, Chapter 1 Pedagogy + Workshop, Nuala Flood and Tristan Sturm, Queen's University Belfast.

between architecture and ANT is symbiotic and that "being independent from the discipline of architecture, it provided a means to describe findings to a multidisciplinary audience and a theory to support the idea that non-human actors, such as water infrastructure, can infer political, social, and economic influence."[9]

Chapter 2 *Pedagogy + Exhibition* examines Elgin Cleckley's work on "_mpathic Design," through the specific case study of two exhibitions created by University of Virginia's School of Architecture, *Mapping* in 2016 and *blue//black* in 2018. Using the mosaic "Design Thinking" methodology, the students worked in interdisciplinary design teams (Architecture, Architectural History, Urban Planning, Education, and Engineering). They began the exhibition process with empathy training, borrowed from the nursing and medical fields and based on two white papers, Dr. Theresa Wiseman's "Concept Analysis of Empathy"[10] and Dr. Helen Reiss and Gordon Kraft-Todd's "E.M.P.A.T.H.Y. A Tool to Enhance Nonverbal Communication."[11] This unique design process allowed the students to understand the subject matter of the exhibitions from a number of other perspectives, therefore, from the outset, designing, building, and reflecting on the exhibition with empathy. The absent e in "_mpathic" symbolises removing personal ego from the design process and "adds an interdisciplinary, action-based understanding of empathy as a platform to overcome cultural differences, bringing marginalized perspectives to the fore."[12]

Milagros Zingoni and Magnus Feil reflect on their collaborative design build project titled "CUMULUS, an inhabitable storm" in Chapter 3 on *Pedagogy + Intervention*, bringing together graduate students in Interior Architecture (IA) and undergraduate students in Industrial Design (ID) from Arizona State University to work alongside young people from a local Title I K-8 school. The chapter discusses the creativity that arises from the social context of a project[13] and argues that "multiple layers of collaboration counteract the prevalent notion that design-build studios hinder creativity due to budget and fabrication constraints."[14] The project used the pedagogic methodology of EDIT (engagement, design, implementation, transformation) which required the students to design and carry out a process of engagement with the local school to inform the design process, to iterate the design and then develop it for implementation, fabricate the final installation (for inclusion in a local festival), and to carry out a post-occupation evaluation. Situated in the wider context of design-build projects, this chapter discusses the community-engaged practices which remind students of their social responsibilities as designers.

Introduction 11

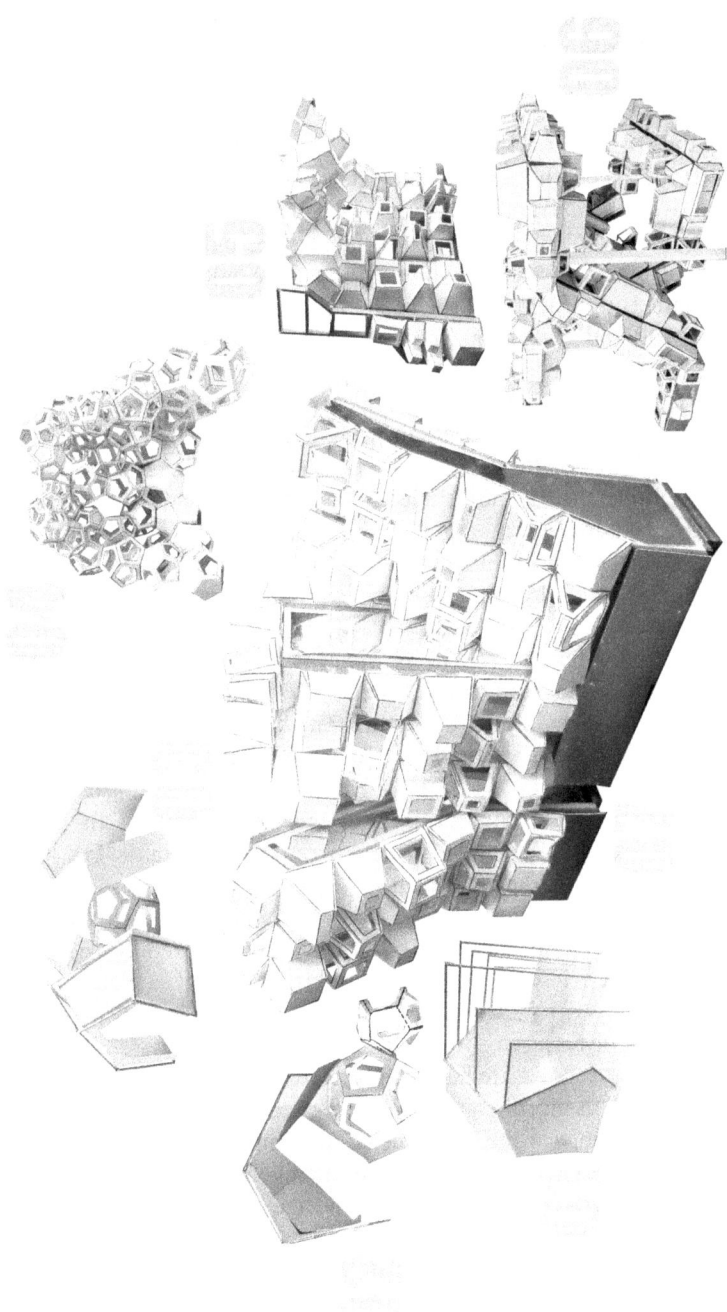

Figure 2 Model iterations, CUMULUS, Chapter 3 Pedagogy + Intervention, Milagros Zingoni and Magnus Feil, Arizona State University.

12 *Sally Stone and Laura Sanderson*

Titled "STEAM & the City," Chapter 4 on *Pedagogy + Production Space* by Alessandro Columbano describes the implementation of STEAMhouse, a production space in Birmingham, a large post-industrial city in the West Midlands of the United Kingdom (UK). Using the critical thinking mechanisms of STEAM, an approach which embeds the arts with "STEM" subjects (science, technology, engineering, and mathematics), the facility is a collaboration between The Birmingham School of Architecture and Design, and Eastside Projects – an artist-led gallery. Drawing on the innovative culture of the city, and its manufacturing heritage, the project highlights that "a creative city requires soft and hard infrastructure to establish a sustainable community of creators and consumers that support the local economy instead of exacerbating rapid urban development and the consequences of gentrification."[15] STEAMhouse is a project (deliberately) located inside an existing building in Digbeth, a redundant industrial area removed from the main university campus. Reflecting on the three years of the project so far, Alessandro Columbano discusses the role that the university has in the physical redevelopment of the city, highlighting STEAMhouse as a sustainable redevelopment (open to the public, for the public), which expands the campus without disenfranchising the existing community.

Our own chapter on *Pedagogy + Policy* (Chapter 5) reflects upon the work of our teaching and research atelier, Continuity in Architecture at the Manchester School of Architecture. Titled "Rochdale Reimagined," the chapter discusses a particular project in the Heritage Action Zone of Rochdale, a large post-industrial town in the north of England, as part of a continuum of collaborative projects. Over a number of years, the atelier has been working closely with different planning teams in the UK. This research began when the UK Localism Bill devolved a series of planning activities to Local Councils or Neighbourhood Planning Committees – a policy which created a series of gaps in both "skill" and "scope." The chapter considers how the "Design Thinking" that takes place in atelier can be applied to local planning problems, drawing on the pedagogic models of research-through-design and problem-based learning. Continuity in Architecture has been concerned with a specific "Wicked Problem" since its inception at Manchester School of Architecture in the 1990s; the challenge of the huge stock of existing buildings and complex "constructed sites"[16] that have outlived the function for which they were built. Their worth is well recognised and the importance of retaining them has been long debated, but if they are to be saved, what is to be done with them?[17] Detailing the collaboration and impact over a number of years, the chapter discusses the role that the architecture school can take in finding a future for the "already built."

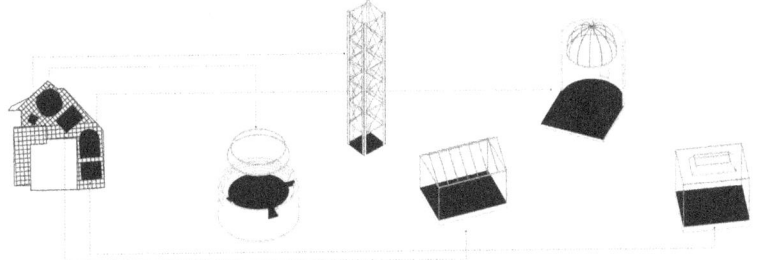

Figure 3 Urban intervention, Courtney Ives + Yiting Zhou, Continuity in Architecture, 2019. Part of "Rochdale Reimagined," Chapter 5 Pedagogy + Policy, Sally Stone and Laura Sanderson, Manchester School of Architecture.

Chapter 6 on *Pedagogy + Resilience* presents the "Designing Resilience in Asia International Research Program" by Oscar Carracedo from the School of Design and Environment at the National University of Singapore. The conceptual framework of the project is based on two publications "Regenerative Development and Design"[18] and "Designing Regenerative Cultures,"[19] which "advocate for a regenerative design, which transforms humanity's impact on Earth from being predominantly destructive to being regenerative, creating a future for humans and all of life by reversing our harmful effects and start to heal communities, ecosystems and the Earth."[20] The project is a laboratory for research and teaching which spans 25 universities, with 400 researchers involved from Asia, Pacific, Europe, Latin America, and North America. The chapter cites a specific example from the DRiA, named "The Synthetic Tree & The Synthetic Forest" by student, Chey Yi Ting, which is a project for carbon negative and nature-positive architecture for Singapore, and argues more broadly that the proposals "critically investigate new forms of urbanism as a relationship between two major triads: on the one hand, ecology, resilience, and sustainability, and on the other hand, culture, space, and urban processes."[21]

These six themes are brought together at a critical time in architectural and design education. As a collection of case studies, they highlight emergent pedagogies which blur the boundary between teaching, design, research, and practice in order to respond to an ever-increasing number of "Wicked Problems".

Notes

1. https://www.delltechnologies.com/content/dam/delltechnologies/assets/perspectives/2030/pdf/SR1940_IFTFforDellTechnologies_Human-Machine_070517_readerhigh-res.pdf [last accessed January 2021].
2. Jones, A., & Hyde, R. *Defining Contemporary Professionalism: For Architects in Practice and Education.* RIBA Publishing, 2019, 127.
3. Jones, A., & Hyde, R. *Defining Contemporary Professionalism: For Architects in Practice and Education.* RIBA Publishing, 2019, 200.
4. Ashraf, M., & Salama, A.M. *Spatial Design Education: New Directions for Pedagogy in Architecture and Beyond.* Routledge, 2015, 12.
5. Ibid, 1.
6. Ibid, 9.
7. Anderson, J., & Priest, C. *Developing an Inclusive Definition, Typological Analysis and Online Resource for Live Projects.* Architecture Live Projects: Pedagogy into Practice, Harriss, H. & Widder, L. [eds], Routledge, 2014, 10.
8. https://architecturemps.com/newyork/ [last accessed January 2021].
9. Flood, N., & Sturm, T. *Chapter 1, Pedagogy + Workshop: 'Public CoLab 2019: Tracing Belfast's Water', 2021.*
10. Wiseman, T. "Concept Analysis of Empathy," *Journal of Advanced Nursing* 23, (1996): 1162-1167
11. Reiss, H., & Kraft-Todd, G. "E.M.P.A.T.H.Y. A Tool to Enhance Nonverbal Communication," *Academic Medicine* 89, no. 8 (2014): 1108-1112
12. Cleckley, E. *Chapter 2, Pedagogy + Exhibition: '_mpathic Design', 2021.*
13. Engeström, Y. "Expansive Learning at Work: Toward an Activity Theoretical Reconceptualization," *Journal of Education and Work* 14, no. 1 (2001): 133–156, DOI: 10.1080/13639080020028747.

14. Zingoni, M., & Magnus, F. *Chapter 3, Pedagogy + Intervention: 'CUMULUS, an inhabitable storm'*, 2021.
15. Columbano, A. *Chapter 4, Pedagogy + Production Space: 'STEAM & the City'*, 2021.
16. Burns, C.J. *On Site: Architectural Preoccupations.* Drawing, Building, Text: Essays in Architectural Theory, Kahn, A. [eds], Princeton Architectural Press, 1991.
17. Stone, S. *UnDoing Buildings: Adaptive Reuse and Cultural Memory.* Routledge, 2019.
18. Haggard, B., & Mang, P. *Regenerative Development and Design: A Framework for Evolving Sustainability.* John Wiley & Sons, Inc., 2016.
19. Wahl, D.C. *Designing Regenerative Cultures*, Permaculture Magazine, 2016.
20. Ibid.
21. Carracedo, O. *Chapter 6, Pedagogy + Resilience: 'Designing Resilience in Asia International Research Program'*, 2021.

1 Pedagogy + workshop

Public CoLab 2019:
Tracing Belfast's water

Nuala Flood and Tristan Sturm

Introduction

This chapter presents a reflection on an architectural pedagogical workshop titled, Public CoLab 2019. It provides an efficient and effective method for understanding the spatial consequences of complex issues of public concern using actor-network theory (ANT) and, more generally, new materialisms as theoretical frameworks. The workshop employed a five-day collaborative live project as the main educational vehicle. Thematically, the students were challenged to understand how water, as an often taken for granted, and yet influential actor in the network of the city, shapes the built environment and lived experience of Belfast, Northern Ireland. Several controversial sub-themes including water scarcity, lead contamination of water, and flooding futures catalysed the workshop and research inquiries. With the help of subject experts from academia, the public sector and charitable organisations, and working in small heterogeneous groups, the students traced the spatiality of a number of affiliated controversies as place-specific and spatial socio-material assemblages. The pedagogical approach was structured to encourage the students to reflect on how they, themselves, are an entangled part of these assemblages. We observed that the workshop participants gained an empirical understanding of how the built environment of the city and its infrastructure can be viewed as an actor-network. In the conclusion, we identify the workshop's effective pedagogical devices and tactics so that this approach can be adapted by other architectural educators with similar goals.

Theoretical positioning

Taking inspiration from Till and his seminal book *Architecture Depends*,[1] the pedagogical approach described in this chapter was created within the context of an anti-modernist reading of architecture as a highly contingent discipline, practice, and product. Architecture, Till suggests, evolves at the nexus of a myriad of interwoven constraints and ontological considerations. He argues: "And with that the notion of the autonomy of architecture should come to a juddering halt. It allows architects to detach themselves as humans (social, political, and ethical beings) and then look through the wrong end of the telescope, and so to see the world as an abstraction. One might think that an abstracted world can be ordered, beautified, and perfected, but in the end the real will come back to bite you. What becomes quickly apparent is that any permanent detachment is deluded."[2] At the human end of the spectrum, demands of clients, planners, users, and the design team all shape the evolution of the architectural brief, and, ultimately, the architectural project. At the non-human end of the spectrum, the physical context, the construction material, the weather, the regulatory framework, and the budget also influence the outcome. Thus, architecture is cultivated by and within an intricate network of human and more-than-human associations.[3]

Corresponding to this view of the practice of architecture as a collaborative and highly contingent endeavour, in recent years there has been a growing interest in using ANT as a methodological framework for understanding the built environment as a complex socio-material assemblage.[4] ANT rejects social, technical, and scientific determinism and reductionism. Rather, it describes the world as a shape-shifting landscape of politically potent human and non-human actors, where technology and society are not ontologically distinct categories; rather, they are co-constitutional with each other.[5] ANT poses that material artefacts, such as buildings, have quasi-agency, and an ability to shape the world in a similar way to people, though they may not operate with precise intentionality. Within this framing of this this project (which decenters the human, and considers them as being part of a larger socio-material assemblage), buildings, as actants, are understood to act in a certain way in reaction to the dynamics of the actor-network.[6] By way of a parallel example, we might think of how COVID-19 as a non-human or more-than-human "thing," has had agency to drastically change our political, economic, and social lives, albeit, without functional intention.[7] Therefore, ANT offers a means of understanding the architectural project as an evolutionary process and an embodiment of a network of associations and relations, that mutate and transform over time.[8,9] ANT has also been deployed to further an understanding of the architectural design and construction process as a multi-player activity, heightening an awareness of how non-human actors, such as drawings and architectural models, exert influence.[10,11,12]

The primary goal of ANT is to reveal or make visible the complex sociotechnical relationships and interactions that have facilitated the construction of technologies we take for granted. Latour denotes this process as opening up a metaphorical "black box," referencing the idea that when a technology is sufficiently mature, established, stable, and efficient, its internal complexity is often ignored. The more successful a technology is, the opaquer its internal workings become; for example, and relevant to our themes in this paper, the *fin de siècle* projects that buried and thus made invisible our water infrastructure and put it in an analogical black box. This led to our water supply, and its chemical constituent parts, to be socially taken for granted. ANT, and other new materialisms theories, wants to expose and make visible this infra(invisible)-structure and trace across scales, what Neimanis calls "bodies of water" – a term that brings into focus the networked ways water, from the body (of which we are 60%) to our infrastructure and landscapes, are bound up and relationally embedded.[13] But more than simply incorporating ANT and new materialisms into architecture, we argue that architecture has much to offer ANT researchers. The deliberate visual and representational focus of architecture can supplement the overly discursive descriptions of human-material networks and relationality. We literally *illustrate* these networked relations in this project and by doing so add to the ANT methodological toolkit.

At the beginning of every design undertaking, the architect must first try and make sense of the complexity inherent in the design's context. Inspired by ANT and the potential that it offers for this task, we created a pedagogical workshop. It aimed to expose students to a design research approach for understanding the city as a socio-material assemblage and a matter of public concern. We aimed to cast new light on common infrastructural and architectural interventions, reframing how the social body conceptualises, respects, and understands our relationship to urban water networks. Tracing actor-networks in architecture has been described as a painstaking and time-consuming task.[14] The workshop sought to address this issue and provide an efficient and effective methodology for this process.[15] Leveraging the benefits of collaboration and taking cues from the idea of a "design sprint,"[16] it took the form of a five-day "live project."[17] Live projects are an established architectural education approach where students engage with real-world contexts, projects, users, and clients.[18] In contrast to more traditional modes of architectural education, where students work from within the confines of the architectural design studio on speculative projects in response to hypothetical briefs, live projects are orientated towards external real-world concerns and, thus, allow the student to engage with practice that resembles professional practice more accurately.[19]

Workshop structure

The aim of the workshop was to examine how water has influenced the development of the built environment and lived experience of Belfast. This theme was chosen because the city's water system – as a place-making device, as a political agent and as a social influencer – can be considered to be a black box or a taken-for-granted technology.[20] Indeed, both urban water and infrastructure have become burgeoning concerns within the theoretical interest in new materialisms and ANT.[21] We challenged the students to explore water as a potentially more-than-human actor that circulates into our bodies via the water infrastructure, manifesting innumerable social, spatial, and cultural consequences. There are many controversial issues associated with the water system in Belfast, and these issues were used to drive the projects and to stimulate the students' interest. Firstly, parts of the city are built along low lying coastal areas and are, therefore, at risk of flooding.[22] This issue will be further exacerbated with global warming, which posits sea-level rise, more severe storms, and increased winter precipitation in Ireland.[23] Conversely, water scarcity also poses threats in Belfast, as was experienced in the heatwave of July 2018, where a hosepipe ban was implemented not because Northern Ireland lacked supply,[24] but because the infrastructure is so old and failing (as is common across the world) that almost 50% of water is lost through leakage before it reaches Belfast.[25] Perhaps most controversially, lead-contaminated water circulates through Belfast unbeknownst to those consuming it. Lead is a neurotoxin, and ingesting it contributes to a host of health problems including reduced IQ, renal issues, and socio-behavioural problems, including violence.[26] Even though lead pipes were legislated out of use in 1969 in the United Kingdom, 34% of houses still have some lead in their drinking water system.[27] This figure is likely to be even higher in Belfast given that approximately 70% of the housing stock in the city precedes this ban, and as a consequence of the Troubles (a thirty-year period of violent unrest in Northern Ireland between 1968 and 1998), much of this water infrastructure has not been renovated to EU public health specifications.[28] Furthermore, there has been a lack of financial incentives made available for private property owners in Northern Ireland to replace their lead pipes.

These provocative issues were used to catalyse the workshop activities and to provide a starting point to critically examine the water infrastructure in Belfast. As such, approximately two months before the intensive five-day workshop, we carried out a priming activity with the student cohort, where they attended a lecture about lead contamination of the water supply by lead pipe infrastructure in Belfast and were offered the opportunity to test their own domestic water supply for lead contamination. The water testing activity revealed that some homes across the city of Belfast had lead levels that exceeded the reference limit of 10 µg/L, indeed one house was nine times higher (93 µg/L). Such high levels put Belfast in the lead level range of the water from Flint, Michigan, whose water supply exposed hundreds of children to the irreversible health effects of lead in 2014.[29] Here students were given a personal, albeit anecdotal, example of how to think using ANT, specifically how their everyday lives were potentially, even likely, influenced by lead exposure in their drinking water. Priming students before the workshop to think about the relationality between their everyday lives and their built environment not only motivated students for the workshop where clear public health consequences of architecture were laid bare, but also crucially gave them the perspective necessary to think about the material world as having a quasi-agency. Several students incorporated this experience into their design research, illustrating the importance of reframing architectural practice for ANT methodologies.

At the five-day workshop, each of the small teams, of between eight and ten first-year undergraduate and first-year master's architecture students, worked with an external expert and a workshop facilitator to explore one of the eight sub-themes: historical water infrastructure, water sources, water scarcity, the modern water pipe network, leaded water contamination, flooding futures, oral cultural histories of the port estuary, and mediating the Lagan River through film. These research areas were established in conversation with these experts and the Department for Infrastructure, NI Water (the public-private company that is responsible for distributing this public resource), Clifton House (the charity that set up the first water supply system in the city), and a number of other academics with relevant knowledge, including oral historians, film-makers, Geographical Information System (GIS) specialists, water scarcity researchers, and climate change visualisers. All of the research work was completed in the shared space of the architecture design studio at Queen's University Belfast. On Monday morning the project was launched and the overarching theme was introduced by way of a theoretical presentation that offered an overview of ANT and contextualising presentations by all of the project partners. The workshop facilitators choreographed a conversation between the teams of students and the external experts in order to mine their knowledge and to explore the research question within the context of Belfast. Desktop, library, and archival research were also undertaken at this stage. On Tuesday the research teams explored their topic and research question in the field. Using survey and observational equipment such as cameras, sketchbooks, and measuring instruments, they recorded how the topic is manifest in the context of public spaces in Belfast, paying particular attention to the visible and hidden relational materiality of water in the city. On Wednesday there was a rapid-fire knowledge sharing session where each of the teams presented the work in progress and initial observations to the entire cohort, the panel of experts, and all of the workshop facilitators. Feedback and reactions to the presentations were offered. The teams then refined their research and questions and made plans for doing further explorations in the field. On Thursday the teams advanced their ideas and began the process of drawing up their conclusions. On Friday morning, the students assembled their findings into a collective output, a zine, titled *Tracing Belfast's Water*, the purpose of which was to trace, make visible, and communicate, to a general public, the buried and taken-for-granted histories, geographies, and architectures of water in Belfast.[30] This work was presented to the entire student cohort, the project partners, and subject experts at a celebratory closing event on Friday afternoon. Below we recount the projects – both their methodology and outputs – via the zine chapters.

The workshop output – the zine – described

The first chapter, *Graphing Archives*, laid the foundation for the entire project. It introduces the topic by way of a graphic and spatial description of the historical founding of the water infrastructure in Belfast. The project partner, Clifton House, is a charitable organisation in Belfast that laid the first water pipes in the city. They provided the students' access to their archives that housed maps and ledgers of this early infrastructure. The students explored how architectural representational tools can be harnessed to describe the state and development of the water infrastructure in the city between 1790 and 1840. Using scaled drawings, diagrams, and photographs, they ground-truthed the historical water infrastructure, as created by Clifton House, mapping it onto the contemporary city of Belfast. This analysis encouraged the students to think about how the modern city of Belfast was made possible – both its built environment and its citizens – via the technological disciplining of nature through the flow of water.[31]

In the next chapter, *Water Scarcity*, the students examined the current water consumption of an average household in Belfast and communicated their findings using infographics, scaling the consumption of the average household to the neighbourhood, city, and state. In so doing the students graphed how three potential future scenarios (based on combination of climate, population, and cultural change) will affect water consumption. Associated with each of these future scenarios, the authors then calculated the water needed for an Ulster Fry (the local breakfast of Northern Ireland) and visualised the water footprint produced in order to meet this demand based on present methods and technologies. Here using architectural representation methods, students thought through and visually realised the intrinsic co-constitution of water and the human body (see Figure 1.1). As a result, this project made visible one of the more effective uses of ANT by linking the scales of water supply to Northern Ireland's food consumption by highlighting the precarity of how our taken-for-granted food networks rely on water.

The next two chapters, *Lead Pipe Water Network (GIS)* and *Leaded Spaces, Leaded Bodies*, explored the paradox of modern water systems: that which nourishes can also poison. The chapter, *Lead Pipe Water Network (GIS)*, asks how QGIS can be utilised to map, visualise, and analyse quantitative data to explore the architectural spatial narrative of water and the city. The authors used collaborative GIS mapping to bring awareness to the amount of lead in the existing water infrastructure and its distribution across space using overlays of historical city maps of water pipe development and the distribution of stopcock covers (metal covers indicate the communication is likely lead). This allowed any public user with a smartphone to map the spatial distribution of lead by assigning nodes to these city infrastructure maps via stopcock identification on the sidewalk. A spatial narrative of water and the city is created through this city scale visualisation. Given that a key agenda for the chapter is awareness of lead via visualisation, the authors created a QR code to help the public map their own lead house pipes.

Inspired by the work on geographies of material politics,[33] *Leaded Spaces, Leaded Bodies* examined the spatial relationship lead has within Belfast. In this chapter, the authors asked: how can architectural representation methods be used to communicate how lead is networked within the built environment of Belfast and within its inhabitant's brains, bones, and blood? They traced how, where, and to what extent the lead network is embedded within the built environment in Belfast but also embodied: how the students were more lead than they knew (see Figure 1.2). They investigated scales of themes ranging from the neighbourhood mapping of lead levels to the surveying of an existing building with high lead levels, to a forensic analysis of the problematic junctions within the existing water supply system to the creation of propositions for a lead-free city. They also mapped networks of how the

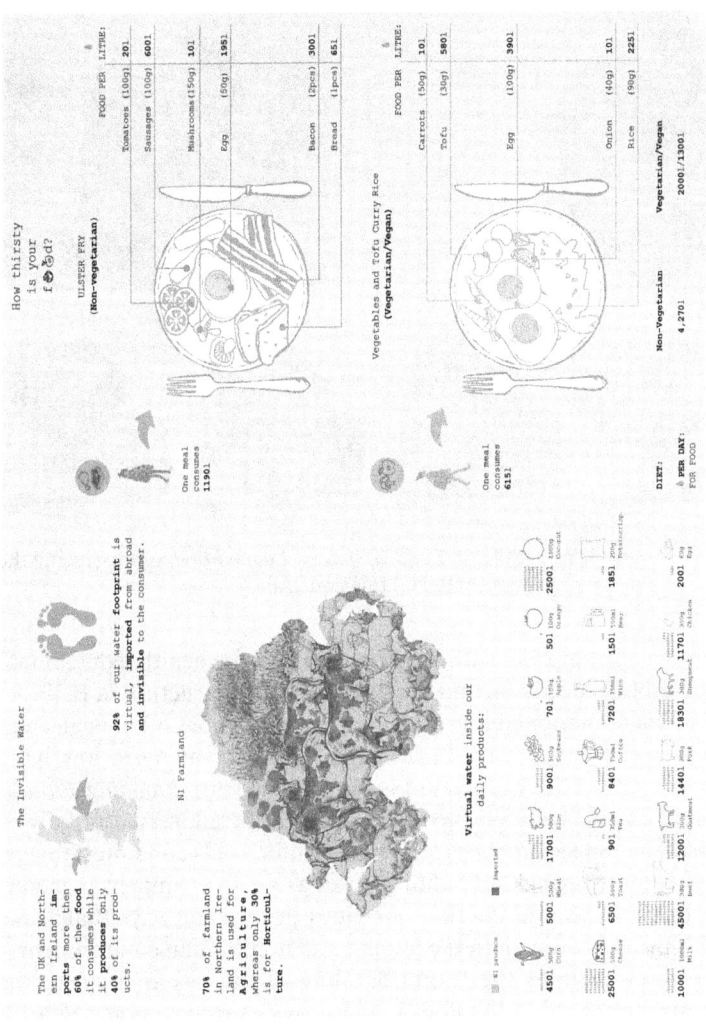

Figure 1.1 Sample spread from water scarcity visualising the water footprint of households in Belfast.

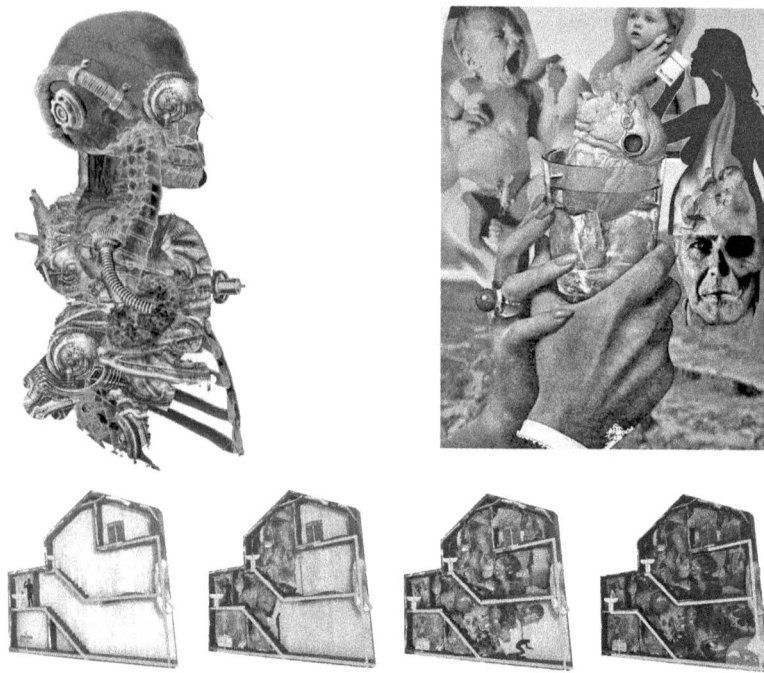

Figure 1.2 Sample images from *Leaded Spaces, Leaded Bodies* illustrating the "cyborg" human-material relationships.[32]

negative health impacts will ultimately impact the health, educational and, possibly, the judicial and social welfare infrastructure in Belfast.

Flooding of inhabited areas is one of the major, but often neglected, challenges that await future generations (and for many in low lying regions of the world, that future is already present). *Flooding Futures* identified a new future problem that needs to be addressed rapidly to help prevent unnecessary loss of lives and unforetold economic damage. But instead of fearing and fighting water as an abject material enemy, some argue we should develop our cities in resilient ways that make use of it by embedding it in the human and non-human environment.[34] This project explores the future flooding of the city of Belfast, the problems correlated to the floods, and provides radical non-defensive solutions. The project asks: what are the predicted problems the city of Belfast will face due to flooding? How can the frame of apocalypse be useful to think through a resilient flooded future? Using the radical anti-colonial historical meaning of "apocalypse" – to unveil the truth – students were asked to think of new architectural millennium – the period after the apocalyptic crisis and therefore after architecture as we know it – that might result from the crisis of urban flooding.[35] In this sense again, water is an actant, having a quasi-agency to affect the human world towards radical change. As was the case in many post-industrial cities, from Baltimore to Sheffield, new urban possibilities opened up from catastrophe for many.[36] From this perspective, we asked what is Belfast's post-urban millennium after the flood? Ultimately the students visualised how architectural thinking and representation, combined with ANT, could be used to explore future flooding scenarios in Belfast. The dominant output of the chapter is a triptych (see Introduction, Figure 1.1) inspired by Hieronymus Bosch's "The Garden of Earthly Delights" (1510) and Thomas Cole's "The Course of Empire" (1933–1936). The triptych of speculative futures for Belfast takes place across three years: 2040, 2062, and 2084.

Oral History along the Lagan explored the interaction between the port and the city of Belfast. The port was revered for its shipbuilding, most famously the Titanic, and was considered a prominent jewel in the British crown, as home to the world's largest and most productive shipyard. The city of Belfast and its prosperity is the direct result of its 19th and early 20th century industrialisation.[37] The deindustrialisation of the 1970s, when the port slipped into an underutilised and undervalued space, radically transforming Belfast's urban landscape. The students investigated the socio-spatial practices of the port and the city through mapping of oral histories and developing a critical interest in the practices of representation, especially in relation to its changing material nature and use: from secondary industry to tertiary neoliberal economies and with it the conversion of industrial landscapes to modern apartments, buildings for finance and call centres, and structures for tourist end entertainment classes.[38] Walking from the Lagan Weir towards the mouth of River Lagan, four spaces were explored through interviews with peripatetic passers-by which included commuters, working-class men, pensioners, tourists, and dog walkers. Here the students explored the effect that the shifting built environment had on the peripatetic subjects. The result maps a varied tapestry of the development and change of the dock areas from a personal perspective. The outcome was a series of sometimes conflicting quotes about the dock areas and a dynamic map illustrating the interactions between the people and the port, their past experiences, and their material engagements. The project is one of becoming with the city and experiencing it from a different, more materially centred position. From the perspective of shoes, students forced a new perspective upon the consumer to look at the river from the subjective perspective of where the interviewees stood *in situ* (see Figure 1.3).

26 Nuala Flood and Tristan Sturm

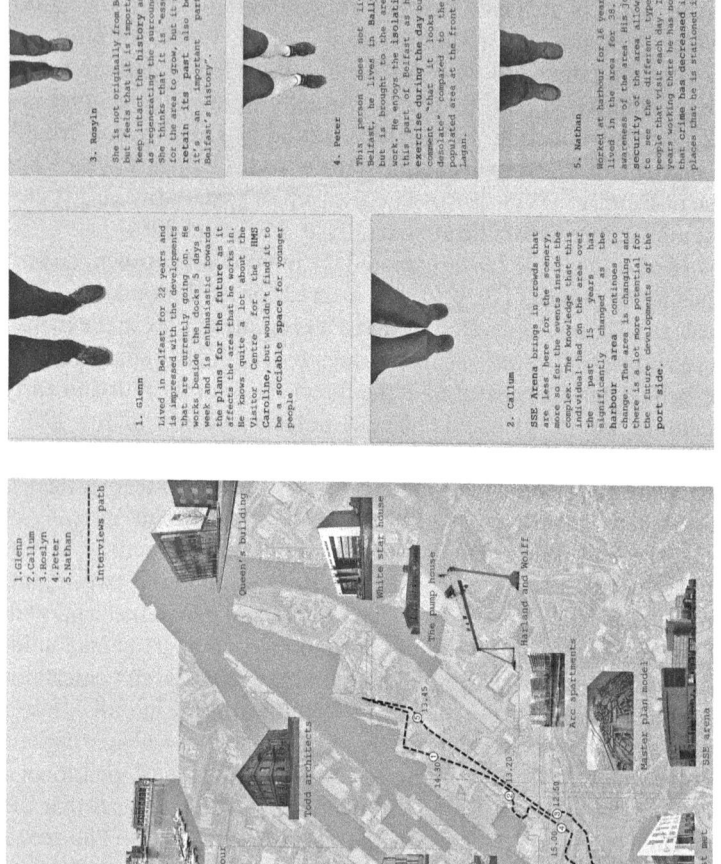

Figure 1.3 Sample spread from Mapping Oral History along the Lagan.

Pedagogy + workshop 27

Water plays and has played a significant role in the landscape of Belfast as a city, via docks, the River Lagan, and indeed the persistent rain that falls on the city due to its geographical location. As such, alongside complaining about the weather, we find that the water's edge is not a celebrated location in the city and instead is solely associated with transit, be it by ferry, car, bicycle, or foot. Through the medium of film, *in Reflections*, the authors attempted to reframe the riverfront as a valuable social and cultural amenity. Water has often played a significant role due to its ability to represent time, due to its fluidity, and its ability to alter the visual content of the image, via reflection, refraction, and transparency. Consequently, throughout the history of film water often becomes an active character that can emphasise both the spatial and emotional content of a scene. For an example of this, one only needs to look at Sergei Eisenstein's early films *Strike* (1925) and *Battleship Potemkin* (1925) both of which use water extensively in a range of different ways where water is more than a stage or backdrop, but rather is deliberately cast as an effective character. Through three short films, two along the Lagan and one in the Silent Valley, the authors explored a range of themes, which included, scale, reflection, refraction, transparency, time, memory, flow, infrastructure, light, form, surface, etc., whilst also exploring different film-making methodologies such as point of view, repetition, narrative, and tracking.

The educational approach reflected upon

The main objective of Public CoLab 2019 was to allow the students to experience an efficient research approach for understanding the spatial implications of complex matters of public concern. The workshop format, as a methodology for this purpose, has been developed and honed over several years using an iterative process of research through pedagogical practice. In previous incarnations, it has been used to explore place-specific consequences of other thorny urban issues such as the relationship between urban design and mental health in the city of Derry, Northern Ireland,[39] and the potential impact of future climate change scenarios in the greater Belfast area.[40] The successive refinement of this pedagogical approach has been informed by feedback from all of the workshop participants – students, academic facilitators, subject experts, and the external collaborators. Based on this action research, the effective tactics used in the workshop are now presented.

In the field of architectural education, project-based learning experiences are rarely positioned within a theoretical framework such as ANT. We observed that this theoretical framing offered many benefits. It provided students, external collaborators, and architectural facilitators a common language with which to discuss water as a political actant. Furthermore, it presented a framework and a shared platform from which to investigate the central theme from several different angles simultaneously. In addition, being independent from the discipline of architecture, it provided a means to describe findings to a multidisciplinary audience and a theory to support the idea that non-human actors, such as water infrastructure, can infer political, social, and economic influence. However, as a means of generating solutions to wicked urban problems, ANT has limitations. Although it prescribes a method of observing, tracing, understanding, and describing actor-networks, it does not attempt to suggest ways of dealing with, acting upon, or designing with the complex socio-material assemblages described. ANT and the new materialisms more generally, then need to be supplemented with more representational praxis-based outcomes. As we argue above, we believe such architectural engagement with ANT intervenes in the theoretical literature and broadens its largely discursive methodological disclosures and descriptions. Therefore, the workshop format might be most usefully deployed at the early stages of a design process, when seeking to cultivate a broad understanding of the design problem.

As a result of attending the contextualising lecture (two months prior to the main workshop) and, subsequently, testing domestic water samples for lead contamination, the students were primed to be critical of the city's water supply system long before participating in the five-day workshop. This priming activity encouraged them to question how they themselves might be ingesting elements of the water infrastructure via lead-contaminated water. More broadly, this leaded controversy acted as a powerful tool for engaging students, for igniting their interest in the subject, and for catalysing the research process as a politically charged inquiry of public concern. Crucially, by carrying out this citizen science activity, they contemplated how they themselves are physically, politically, culturally, and cerebrally entangled with the water infrastructure and, by association, with the city.

The structure of Public CoLab 2019 presented numerous opportunities for generating a relational understanding of the overarching topic, with cross-learning events woven throughout the format. Firstly, at the launch of the workshop, all of the project collaborators presented their research questions and themes, allowing all of the students to develop an awareness of all of the other individual projects. Secondly, a knowledge sharing session was facilitated halfway through the workshop, where the students shared an overview of their work in progress. This session provided a further opportunity for developing familiarity with all the other sub-themes. We found this cross-pollination of research findings and mediums pushed the students and had a motivational effect, creating more advanced outputs. Thirdly, the students worked from the shared space of the design studio. This communal research setting promoted casual conversations and chance encounters between different student groups, academic facilitators, and subject experts which, thus, supported the further generation of other relational understandings of the topic. Fourth, the common goal of producing the zine, offered yet another opportunity for cross-learning. And finally, the diverse and multidisciplinary input also supported the generation of a multifaceted and relational understanding of the overarching topic.

The transdisciplinary conceptualisation of the project was driven from the outset, with one of the curators (Tristan Sturm) being a geographer and the other curator (Nuala Flood) being an architect. This transdisciplinary collaboration encouraged us to look further afield, challenging the boundaries of architecture to include collaborators from different disciplinary and vocational backgrounds (oral history, film-making, photography, engineering, GIS, and climate science). The architectural facilitators (Chantelle Niblock, Seán Cullen, Niek Turner, and Jasna Mariotti) managed their teams by summarising their discussions and helped link the studio culture to the field experts (who were from non-architectural backgrounds). Translating the architectural experience from, and to, the external experts provided an effective way of bringing their expertise to the project, which catalysed the projects, and gave direction based on their deep knowledge of the subject areas. In addition, we observed that the transdisciplinary nature of the project encouraged the generation of new findings, fresh insights, and offered new learning opportunities. For instance, the students merged oral history, walking interviews, photography, and mapping methods to produce an innovative description of water bodies as a place-making devices in Belfast.

We also observed that the research teams profited from having the input of both the novice stage 1 architecture student, with their unassuming attitude towards what architectural research could be, and the more experienced master's student. The stage 1 students offered fresh perspective and innovative thinking, as demonstrated in the development of the participatory mapping application, while the master's students had more diverse and developed research and graphic representational skills to bring to the projects. This experiential diversity of ontological and epistemological perspectives meant the un-"disciplined" undergraduates could bring their broader thinking of what was possible in architecture to bear on the thematic canvas, bringing multiple conceptualisations into view. For the postgraduates, as one imparted to us of the experience, "I thought this project was going to be a caretaking or tutor role with the first years, but in the end this project has expanded my endeavours in architectural design to think beyond the building." The result of such collaborative *esprit de corps* was, as Brown, Harris, and Russell recently put it, "solving wicked problems with the transdisciplinary imagination."[41] The mixing of such diverse disciplinary and educational level should also be a reminder of how our architectural epistemologies can build limiting borders around the discipline.

The benefits of looking at the idea of the water-body network at different scales, the molecular, the human scale, the house, neighbourhood, city, region, and global scale (in water scarcity), meant that the issue was seen from multiple vantage points, generating a more holistic and networked understanding of the issue, "scale bending" the analysis. Instead of scale defining the boundaries of analysis and thus locking in a stratified focus, the threads of analysis that run across and through scales of analysis are "systematically challenged and upset …. entrenched assumptions about what kinds of social activities fit properly at which scales."[42] Scale bending can lead to underdetermined findings and fuzzy logics, but with the methodological demand of ANT to trace all contributing human and non-human factors, the analysis was held together and justified by the theory itself.

Given the broad scope and scale of the topics explored in Public CoLab 2019 and the multiple disciplines involved in the event, there was potential for the research process to become unwieldy. We mitigated this by using several tactics to constrain the research explorations. For instance, the limited five-day time intensive session was beneficial in that it compelled the students to focus their investigations. In addition, all of the research investigations were anchored in the same physical location, Belfast. This place-based constraint also benefitted the development of a relational understanding, providing a common reference point for all projects.

Conclusion

Neimanis' concept of "bodies of water" brings into relief and theorises the ways in which taken-for-granted materials of everyday life, in this case water, have a quasi-agency, affecting not only humans but also their own relationally scaled worlds.[43] She muses upon this: "Today, when you or I drink a glass of water, we amplify this Hypersea, as we sustain our existence through other 'webs of physical intimacy and fluid exchange' .... we connect with the sedimentation tanks, and rapid-mix flocculators that make that water drinkable, and the reservoir, and the rainclouds, too …. To drink a glass of water is to ingest the ghosts of bodies that haunt that water."[44] Water can be conceptualised by what some scholars of space have called "more-than-human" actors.[45] By having students trace the network of those actors or actants (those *bodies* of water) they come to recognise how their lives are relationally bound with the material water, architecturally, geographically, and otherwise.[46] Our students brought into relief graphically those ghosts that haunt water, how humans are not the humanist masters of the world, but are rather de-centred and relationally made up by our natural and built environments. More generally, as a result of mapping the water network in Belfast, our students developed an empirical understanding of how the city can be seen as a sociomaterial assemblage of human and non-human actors. The hope is that they are now equipped with a more nuanced, expansive, and multifaceted understanding of the city, along with new methodological competencies to understand other complex design contexts.

We acknowledge that the collective output, the zine, offers a multifaceted, rather than a comprehensive, description of water and water infrastructure in Belfast. There were gaps in the research that were not possible to address given the available expertise, limited resources, and time constraints of the project. However, the workshop format described in this chapter demonstrates how transdisciplinary collaboration can be leveraged to generate a broad understanding of a complex topic in a very short period. The facilitators aided diverse team members to work together effectively by clearly defining tasks, goals, and work schedules, while simultaneously ensuring that all team members have scope to contribute to the knowledge generation process. As a result of making the topic personal, through the testing of the domestic water samples, all team members were intellectually invested in the process from the outset of the project. The collective relational understanding of the topic was further deepened by continuously sharing the emergent findings throughout the duration of the workshop. Moreover, having ANT as a common theoretical framework helped to link each of the different topics.

Public CoLab 2019 demonstrates how ANT offers an apt conceptualisation and framing of the world to support the more representational practice of architecture as a highly contingent undertaking and a language for communicating the multiple social and spatial consequences of complex matters of public concern. However, the focus of ANT is describing and cultivating and understanding of complex matters of public concern. It does not suggest ways of generating solutions, a path forward or a way of working within this complexity. Therefore, there are limitations in using ANT as generative device. Moreover, we see ANT as a framing that supplements the core ocular centric representation practices of architecture, rather than replacing it. Because of this, we argue that architectural practice can push the boundaries of ANT by encouraging spatial design and visualisation. It can, therefore, be concluded that it might be best deployed at the early stages of the design process when seeking to understand the design space.

We hope that the disclosure of our Public CoLab 2019 theories, methodology, and practice provides a toolkit, albeit open-ended, for other themes to be explored by architecture schools. For example, given the COVID-19 pandemic, architecture students might be encouraged to think of how air, specifically its flow and volume in urban and architectural places/spaces, is networked.[47] Asking students to trace and make visible air, both aesthetically and as a social agent, and as a taken-for-granted yet ubiquitous "thing", is an effective vehicle in the design process is potentially a challenging and instructive vehicle for learning.

Acknowledgements

The authors would like to thank the supporting organisations – Water NI, the Department for Infrastructure and Clifton House – for contributing to the project. We are also thankful to the academic facilitators, Dr. Jasna Mariotti, Dr. Chantelle Niblock, Dr. Niek Turner, and Dr. Sean Cullen for their creative contributions. We are also thankful to the subject experts – Prof. Sean O'Connell, Prof. Greg Keeffe, Dr. Siobhan McDermott, Mr. Stephen Mulhall, Mr. Aaron McIntyre, and Ms. Rebecca Jane McConnell – for partaking in the collaborative investigation. We are grateful to all the hard-working students for participating wholeheartedly in the project and to the reviewers of this chapter for their valuable feedback. We would also like to thank the Architecture Programme at Queen's University Belfast as well as the Culture & Society research group in the School of Natural and Built Environment for funding the testing of participants' domestic water samples.

Notes

1. Jeremy Till, *Architecture Depends* (Cambridge: MIT Press, 2009).
2. Jeremy Till, *Architecture Depends* (Cambridge: MIT Press, 2009), 25.

3. Tommaso Venturini, "Building on Faults: How to Represent Controversies with Digital Methods," *Public Understanding of Science* 21 (2012): 796–812; Bruce Braun, "Environmental Issues: Writing a More-than-Human Urban Geography," *Progress in Human Geography* 29 (2005): 635–650.
4. Bruno Latour, "A Cautious Prometheus? A Few Steps toward a Philosophy of Design (with Special Attention to Peter Sloterdijk)," *Sciences-Po* 03/09, 2008.
5. Bruno Latour, *Reassembling the Social: An Introduction to Actor-Network-Theory* (Oxford: Oxford University Press, 2005).
6. Cristiano Storni, "Notes on ANT for Designers: Ontological, Methodological and Epistemological Turn in Collaborative Design," *CoDesign* 11 (2015): 166–178.
7. Bruce Braun, "Biopolitics and the molecularization of life," *Cultural Geographies* 14 (2007): 6–28.
8. Bruno Latour and Albena Yaneva, "Give Me a Gun and I will Make All Buildings Move: An ANT's View of Architecture," in *Explorations in Architecture: Teaching, Design, Research*, ed. Reto Geiser (Basel: Birkhauser, 2008), 80–89.
9. Kjetil Fallan, "Architecture in Action: Traveling with Actor-Network Theory in the Land of Architectural Research," *Architectural Theory Review* 13 (2008): 80–96.
10. Albena Yaneva and Liam Heaphy, "Urban Controversies and the Making of the Social," *Arq: Architectural Research Quarterly* 16 (2012): 29–36.
11. Albena Yaneva, *Mapping Controversies in Architecture* (Abingdon: Routledge, 2016).
12. Albena Yaneva, *Made by the Office for Metropolitan Architecture: An Ethnography of Design* (Rotterdam: 010 Publishers, 2009).
13. Astrida Neimanis, *Bodies of Water: Posthuman Feminist Phenomenology* (London: Bloomsbury, 2017).
14. Albena Yaneva, *Mapping Controversies in Architecture* (Abingdon: Routledge, 2016).
15. Vinícius Gomes Ferreira and Edna Dias Canedo, "Design Sprint in Classroom: Exploring New Active Learning Tools for Project-Based Learning Approach," *Journal of Ambient Intelligence and Humanized Computing* 11 (2020): 1191–1212.
16. Jake Knapp, *Sprint: How to Solve Big Problems and Test New Ideas in just Five Days* (Random House, 2016).
17. Harriet Harriss and Lynnette Widder, *Architecture Live Projects: Pedagogy into Practice* (Abingdon: Routledge, 2014).
18. Melanie Dodd and Fiona Harrisson, "Defining Live Projects," in *Live Projects: Designing with People*, eds. Esther Charlesworth, Melanie Dodd, and Fiona Harrisson (Melbourne: RMIT University Press, 2012), 2–3.
19. Nuala Flood, "Let the Power of Live Projects Combine," *Iterations: Design Research and Practice Review* 4 (2016): 8–15.
20. Iain White, *Water and the City: Risk, Resilience and Planning for a Sustainable Future* (Abingdon: Routledge, 2013); David Sedlak, *Water 4.0: The Past, Present, and Future of the World's most Vital Resource* (New Haven: Yale University Press, 2014).

21. Nikhil Anand, *Hydraulic City: Water and the Infrastructures of Citizenship in Mumbai* (Durham: Duke University Press, 2017); Karen Bakker and Gavin Bridge, "Material Worlds? Resource Geographies and the 'Matter of Nature'," *Progress in Human Geography* 30 (2006): 5–27; Shiloh Deitz and Katie Meehan, "Plumbing Poverty: Mapping Hot Spots of Racial and Geographic Inequality in US Household Water Insecurity," *Annals of the American Association of Geographers*, 109 (2019): 1092–1109.
22. "Flood Maps NI," accessed 01/11, 2018, http://dfi-ni.maps.arcgis.com/apps/webappviewer/index.html?id=fd6c0a01b07840269a50a2f596b3daf6.
23. The Met Office, *UKCP18 Science Overview – Executive Summary*, 2018.
24. BBC, "Hosepipe Ban Introduced Amid Heatwave," last modified 30/06, accessed 14/08, 2019, https://www.bbc.co.uk/news/uk-northern-ireland-44651240.
25. Nikhil Anand, Akhil Gupta, and Hannah Appel (eds.), *The Promise of Infrastructure* (Durham: Duke University Press, 2018).
26. Gerald Markowitz and David Rosner, *Lead Wars: The Politics of Science and the Fate of America's Children* (Berkeley: University of California Press, 2014); Mona Hanna-Attisha, *What the Eyes Don't See – A Story of Crisis, Resistance, and Hope in an American City* (New York: Random House, 2018).
27. Werner Troesken, *The Great Lead Water Pipe Disaster* (Cambridge: MIT Press, 2006); Steve Potter, *Lead in Drinking Water* (London: House of Commons Library Research, 1997).
28. Liam O'Dowd and Milena Komarova, "Contesting Territorial Fixity? A Case Study of Regeneration in Belfast," *Urban Studies* 48 (2011): 2013–2028.
29. Mona Hanna-Attisha, *What the Eyes Don't See: A Story Of Crisis, Resistance, and Hope In An American City* (New York: Random House, 2018).
30. Nuala Flood and Tristan Sturm, *Tracing Belfast's Water* (Belfast: Queen's Architectural Press, 2020).
31. On water infrastructure making the "modern" city, see Matthew Gandy, *The Fabric of Space Water, Modernity, and the Urban Imagination* (Cambridge: MIT Press, 2014).
32. Donna Haraway, *Simians, Cyborgs, and Women: The Reinvention of Nature* (New York: Routledge, 1991)
33. Andrew Barry, *Material Politics: Disputes along the Pipeline* (Chichester: Wiley-Blackwell, 2013); Bruce Braun and Sarah J. Whatmore (eds.), *Political Matter: Technoscience, Democracy, and Public Life* (Minneapolis: University of Minnesota Press, 2010).
34. Johan Rockström et al., *Water Resilience for Human Prosperity* (Cambridge: Cambridge University Press, 2014).
35. Tristan Sturm and Jason Dittmer, "Introduction," in *Mapping the End Times: American Evangelical Geopolitics and Apocalyptic Visions*, eds. Jason Dittmer and Tristan Sturm (Abingdon: Routledge, 2016), 1–23; Nick Megoran "Radical politics and the Apocalypse: activist readings of Revelation," *Area* 45 (2013): 141–147.
36. J. K. Gibson-Graham, *A Postcapitalist Politics* (Minneapolis: University of Minnesota Press, 2006), 1–22.

37. Fredrick Boal and Stephen Royle, *Enduring City* (Belfast: Blackstaff Press, 2006).
38. David Harvey, *The Condition of Postmodernity: An Enquiry into the Origins of Cultural Change* (Malden: Blackwell, 1989).
39. Nuala Flood, "Public CoLab 2018: Enlivening the riverfront in Derry-Londonderry," *Architecture Ireland* 308 (2019): 72–73.
40. Nuala Flood and Don Duncan, *Public CoLab 2020: Exploring the Impact of the Ecological Crisis in Belfast* (Issu, 2020).
41. Valerie A. Brown, John A. Harris, and Jacqueline Y. Russell, *Tackling Wicked Problems: Through the Transdisciplinary Imagination* (Abingdon: Routledge, 2010); Sanda Lenzholzer and Robert D. Brown, "Post-positivist Microclimatic Urban Design Research: A Review," *Landscape and Urban Planning* 153 (2016): 111–121.
42. Neil Smith "Scale Bending and the Fate of the National" in *Scale and Geo-graphic Inquiry,* eds. Eric Sheppard and Robert McMaster 192–212 (Malden: Blackwell, 2004), 193.
43. Astrida Neimanis, *Bodies of Water: Posthuman Feminist Phenomenology* (London: Bloomsbury, 2017).
44. Astrida Neimanis, "Hydrofeminism: Or, On Becoming a Body of Water" in *Undutiful Daughters: Mobilizing Future Concepts, Bodies and Subjectivities in Feminist Thought and Practice,* eds. Henriette Gunkel, Chrysanthi Nigianni, and Fanny Söderbäck (New York: Palgrave Macmillan, 2012), 97–98.
45. Adrian Franklin, "The More-than-Human City," *The Sociological Review* 65 (2017): 202–217.
46. Julian S Yates, Leila M Harris, and Nicole J Wilson, "Multiple ontologies of water: Politics, conflict and implications for governance," *Environment and Planning D: Society and Space* 35 (2017): 797–815.
47. Kimberley Peters and Philip Steinberg, "Volume and Vision: Fluid Frames of Thinking Ocean Space," *Harvard Design Magazine* 35 (2014): 124–129; Stuart Elden, "Secure the volume: Vertical geopolitics and the depth of power," *Political Geography* 34 (2013): 35–51.

2 Pedagogy + exhibition
_mpathic design

Elgin Cleckley

Introduction

Designing with empathy is of urgent importance in today's design education, as students seek inclusive methodologies in response to systemic inequalities exposed in 2020s health and racial justice pandemics. Entering an even more complex world post academy requires the essential development of a designer's ethics and aesthetics. _mpathic design (the absent e symbolizing removing one's ego in the design process) is a model for this moment – an award-winning pedagogy, initiative, and design practice established at the University of Virginia's School of Architecture. _mpathic design's action-oriented empathic Design Thinking methodology, the *mosaic*, incorporates thirty years of academic, professional, and community design justice work on identity, culture, memory, history, and place. This chapter details _mpathic design's inspirations and influences, principles, and methods, exampled in two student-led exhibitions. The complex cultural landscape of Central Virginia, and Thomas Jefferson's Academical Village, supplies an example for design operation, meeting essential student, community, and faculty aspirations of inclusion and equity. _mpathic design operates in the UVa School of Architecture's Design Thinking curriculum, where Design Thinking is defined as the systematic, rigorous methodologies, and modes of inquiry used by designers. _mpathic design adds an interdisciplinary, action-based understanding of empathy as a platform to overcome cultural differences, bringing marginalized perspectives to the fore.

_mpathic design: Inspirations and influences

Inspirations and influences for _mpathic design began in the 1970s, starting with the authors' interest in African American patchwork quilts, imagining them as plan, section, and elevation. The quilts act as

DOI: 10.4324/9781003174080-2

empathy devices, with each patch holding a narrative of the plantation histories of the author's native South Carolina.[1] These same quilts provided comfort during *The Great Migration* (the exodus of blacks from the south to the north from 1910 to 1970, seeking escape from the racial terror of Jim Crow) to arrive in the urban fabric of New York City.[2] In Harlem, the dynamic collage work of Romare Bearden, representing scale, experience, and culture, provides another foundational African American empathy device.[3] Romare Bearden, Charles Alston, Emma Amos, Norman Lewis, and Hale Woodruff formed the Spiral Group, a New York-based African American artists' collective active from 1963 to 1965, collaborating as an interdisciplinary group of empathic design thinkers.[4] The Studio Museum of Harlem notes the collective's fundamental empathic design questions: *are aesthetic sensibilities specific to racial identity? What relationship should artists have with the social and political concerns of black Americans?*[5] _mpathic design models this collaboration – exploring the relationship of art (design) and activism, essential for the current sociocultural movement.

As a student of the University of Virginia's School of Architecture beginning in 1989, _mpathic design wrestled with the purposely absent narrative of enslaved African Americans in Thomas Jefferson's Academical Village. Architectural History curriculums ignored the construction of the Academical Village by the enslaved, ignoring the plantation's work camps' existence in its lush floral gardens. The garden wall's famous serpentine walls were higher – designed by Jefferson (and built by the enslaved) – to hide slaves. Students now know the truth of the violence the enslaved endured by students and faculty alike when experiencing the empathic design of the Memorial to Enslaved Laborers, along with tours and exhibitions in the central Rotunda.[6] Karla McLaren, the creator of the term empath, defines the empathy found in these designs, putting into form the "social and emotional skill that helps us feel and understand the emotions, circumstances, intentions, thoughts, and needs of others, such that we can offer sensitive, perceptive, and appropriate communication and support." McLaren continues to detail the effect of these new empathic designs, stating that "empathy helps us re-engage with public spaces and read anew the nuances, subtexts, undercurrents, intentions, thoughts that structure social space."[7]

Empathic background: Practice

_mpathic design continued to emerge through professional practice, designing educational facilities in Southwest Washington State in collaborations with DLR Group from 1995 to 1997. These educational facilities' designs emerged from curated empathic community interviews, resulting in designs utilizing materials produced from local economies. Continuing in Chicago's West Side in 1997, the renovation and conversion of industrial sites reintroduced historical narratives, before joining Toronto's Baird Sampson Neuert Architects (BSN), where form and function developed sociocultural driven mausoleum designs. Empathy skills expanded in a role as the Design Coordinator and 3D Group Leader at the Ontario Science Centre (OSC) from 2001 to 2016, producing architecture, exhibitions, and the world's first Design Thinking facility, the *Weston Family Innovation Centre*. At the OSC, all design incorporates the *cultural mosaic*, coined by John Murray Gibbon, author of *Canadian Mosaic: The Making of a Northern Nation*, as the mix of ethnic groups, languages, and cultures that coexist within society. _mpathic design's core methodology, the *mosaic*, contains methods that accept one's characteristics and heritage (as a piece in metaphorical *mosaic*), instead of the impossible "melting pot" metaphor long held in the United States.[8]

In current practice, _mpathic design leads Design + Thinking Workshops with the City of Lynchburg, Virginia's Dearington Neighborhood Plan (an African American community), commemorating a pool closed to prevent integration while providing restorative design elements for its central hub, Jefferson Park. In 2019, _mpathic design provided site planning for the John Henry James Memorial in Court Square, Charlottesville, where a Confederate soldier statue installed in 1909, was recently voted to be removed by Albemarle County in August 2020. The James Memorial originates from the Equal Justice Initiative of Montgomery, Alabama's National Memorial Peace and Justice, by Bryan Stevenson and MASS Design Group. James, an African American man accused of assault of Julia Hottopp, a white woman from a prominent Charlottesville family, occurred in 1898.[9] Visitors to Court Square learn of James' lynching just west of Charlottesville, where he was taken off of a train from nearby Staunton (kept for safety from white mobs gathered outside the Court House jail), hung from a tree, and shot more than 40 times, with pieces of his clothing taken as souvenirs. The memorial marks the first time in the City's history that an African American's life is told in a representational form in a public square.

_mpathic design: Principles

Early research focused on empathy skills developed by the design company IDEO, where Design Thinking "relies on the human ability to be intuitive, to recognize patterns, and to construct ideas that are emotionally meaningful as well as functional."[10] IDEO uses empathy maps as a brainstorming tool to record what consumers say and do, designers project what users think and feel. _mpathic design and the *mosaic* recognize these aspects as foundational, while incorporating political scientist and economist Herbert A. Simon's definition that the action of design is to "devise *courses of action* aimed at changing existing situations into preferred ones."[11] Hybridically, the *mosaic* introduces empathic *courses of action* to help overcome the *wicked problems* (heightened in our current racial justice climate), as noted by Design Theorist Horst Rittel.[12] _mpathic design imports Susan Lanzoni's (historian of psychology, psychiatry, and neuroscience) definition of empathy, as "our capacity to grasp and understand the mental and emotional lives of others," "variably deemed a trained skill, a talent, or an inborn ability."[13] Lanzoni's definition takes hold in Jefferson's Academical Village, evolving into two principles. **Principle 1**, *your embodiment in a space*, cites architect and humanist Robert Lamb Hart. Hart states that "we read relationships between buildings, landscapes, and streetscapes in social terms, too, imagining their dialogues and conflicts and sensing them rejecting or welcoming us, almost like a family member or a friend."[14] **Principle 2**, *Einfühlung* – an aesthetic *(feeling into)*, is a dialogical act of projecting oneself into another body or environment. *In – feeling* (from Lanzoni – citing German philosophers Theodor Lipps and Robert Vischer), captures projection of feeling and movement into paintings, objects of art (extending to architecture), and nature.

The methodology: The mosaic

Exhibition example 1

Mapping

_mpathic design developed *Mapping* in 2016, led by the *mosaic*. This section details the stages/process of the method (highlighted in bold). *Mapping* consists of fragment representation of a Pavilion roof form, evoking the ten Pavilions of Jefferson's Academical Village. The roof form includes three slate tiles made (once installed) by the enslaved in the 1800s at its top, with slate tiles removed from the West Range in 2016 in rows below. Surrounding the roof form in the West Oval Room (on the main floor of the Rotunda) are a series of graphic panels displaying the empathic tour provided in the UVa Walking Tour brochure on Enslaved African Americans at the University of Virginia.[15]

The mosaic: Stage 1 – empathic discovery

Mapping began with discovering the Walking Tour for Enslaved African Americans in the exhibition on the University (installed in 2016) in the Lower East Oval Room of the Rotunda.[16] Here, visitors experience a series of interactives, informing, for the first time, the lives of the enslaved who built the University. These exhibitions inform visitors of 1817, when Jefferson marked the locations for the buildings with overseer Edmund Bacon, and Irish builder James Dinsmore, with ten enslaved "hands."[17]

The *mosaic* begins by the instructor **strategically creating diverse, interdisciplinary design teams** with Architecture, Architectural History, Urban Planning, Education, and Engineering students. Students receive **empathy training** through white papers from the nursing and medical fields, used in _mpathic design's academic, community, and professional contexts. The papers supply students with relatable, interactive examples of empathy-building in action. The first paper, nursing scholar Dr. Theresa Wiseman's *Concept Analysis of Empathy*, details empathy as *seeing the world as others see it (perspective), being non-judgmental, understanding another's feelings, and communicating the knowledge*. The second white paper, Dr. Helen Reiss' and Gordon Kraft-Todd's *E.M.P.A.T.H.Y., A Tool to Enhance Nonverbal Communication Between Clinicians and Their Patients*, uses the letters of empathy as a guide (E for Eye contact, M – Muscles of Facial Expression, P – Posture, A – Affect, T – Tone of voice, H – Hearing, and Y – Your response).[18] Students learn of **Design Thinking logic** through *Design Thinking and Its application* from Kees Dorst, Professor of Design Innovation at the University of Technology, Sydney. Dorst states that designers utilize Abduction, a basic reasoning pattern for productive thinking, with the following equation: *WHAT (thing) + HOW (the working principle) leading to = VALUE (aspired)*. Following Dorst, the team determined: *VALUE* of what we wish to create (telling the narrative of the enslaved at UVa), the *HOW* – a "working principle" that will help achieve value (creating an exhibition that puts you, the visitor, in the place of the Builder, the enslaved), defining the *WHAT* – an object, a service, a system – (the roof form exhibition, and adjacent panels).

Students **analyse stakeholders through an empathy lens** in design teams, creating a list of core, direct, and indirect stakeholders, mirroring practices from the instructor's professional design experience. Questions such as: *what do I want (the selected identity) to know (experiencing the exhibition for each stakeholder)? What do I want (the selected* *identity) to feel? What do I want (the selected identity) to understand? How will I know that the Design is making an impact (for the selected identity)? Who are those that would not like, believe, or disagree with the information presented in this design? How can we still connect with them?*

Design teams **set project goals and objectives**, thinking of how the exhibition can connect with all audiences, considering those in support, and resistors to the legacies of slavery at the University. This exercise includes role-playing of stakeholders in group discussions. Stage 1 concludes with an **empathy tour**, walking the Academical Village in the hot summer sun, after reading accounts of the enslaved from the research that the President's Commission on Slavery and the University, imagining what it took for the enslaved to build the University.[19]

The mosaic: Stage 2 – experiential designing and making

The student team heads into *five identifiable stages in the sequence of designing and making*, citing British author, scholar, and architect Patrick Nuttgens.[20] The first is **Identification: discovery or recognition of needs**, where students analyse visitors, inquiring with administrative staff of the West Oval Room of the Rotunda. Research of the demographics and racial makeup of students, faculty, and visitors (local, national, and international) are added while reviewing the existing empathic nature of the Rotunda's exhibitions. (Figure 2.1) Second is **Collection: of information, assembly of facts**, researching the architecture of the Pavilions of the Academical Village, contacting UVa facilities management, and finding the original slate from the enslaved, while collecting discarded slate from the West Range. Research in this Stage extends to researching original construction drawings of the Pavilions to make the fragmented Pavilion roof form. **Analysis: of those needs and facts** follows third, with extensive discussions emerging into the *Body and the Builder* concept, empathically placing visitors in the place of the enslaved builders, imagining conditions in the hot Virginia sun (following lessons from the *Empathy Tour*). The "hand" of the *Builder* becomes etching of the slate of the University map, with fabrication echoing building construction of the time (as noted by engineering student Rosalie Reuss), developing into designs to show voids for where the beams would be, placement and cuts evoking the 1800s.[21] Synthesis at this point of the process continued to form the *Body and the Builder* concept – with visitors to the exhibition approaching the fragmented roof form, realizing the slate is arranged the opposite way as the Pavilions one sees at the Academical Village. Principles 1 and 2

Figure 2.1 Mapping exhibition, on display in the Rotunda, West Oval Room (Graphic Panels, and "Pavilion" roof form).

are present in this design concept – requiring visitors to understand the enslaved view from on top of the roof, touching a historical timeline of slate. Fourth is **Idea: the new potential thing that exists, or will exist, to bring together and make into one the needs, techniques, demands, and means.** This Stage includes prototyping and production of the fragmented roof form, design of the Graphic Panels from the Walking Tour, laser etching the University map into the slate. The final, fifth Stage is **Realization: things take shape, work, or fail. Fail, you may go back to further thought and analysis.** Installation in the West Oval room, as the exhibition takes shape, includes adding lighting underneath the roof form to provide an anti-gravity effect. In this Stage, student discussions result in the exhibition's strategic placement in the sightlines from the main entrance of the Rotunda, just off the axis of its Jefferson statue.

The mosaic: Stage 3 – empathic implementation

Stage 3 focuses on the effect of an empathic design placed into built environments and cultural landscapes. This Stage includes implementation planning, with students discussing appropriate locations for the exhibition on the University grounds. Students create talking points for discussion with administrators to place the exhibition in its iconic location, connoting impacts on studied stakeholders, receiving approval to install in the West Oval Room, just one floor up. Administrators and staff learn from the student design team the required location for the West Oval Room exhibition to share with all who visit. Thinking of visitor experience leads Stage 3, as the exhibition sites near windows, for views toward the Lawn, allowing visitors to look at the fragmented roof form, turning around to view the room itself, seeing the same materials installed by the enslaved. This Stage continues into empathic conversations with University Student Guides, colleagues of members of the design team, marking the exhibition as a location for starting tours of the Academical Village.

Mapping: Closing notes

Mapping's fabrication halted due to the Unite the Right white supremacy rally and events of August 11 and 12, 2017. A member of the design team was injured in a peaceful protest in the car attack that killed Heather Heyer by James Fields on August 12. These events ceased work for a significant recovery period yet charged our contribution to racial justice design in this context.

Mapping received a Jefferson Trust Grant, a research grant from the School of Architecture, and the 2020 ACSA Diversity Achievement Award. The exhibition was integral in the school's 2019 Graduate School's Inclusion and Equity Open House, resulting in the largest increase in African American students in the school's history. *Mapping* completed its tour, with a display at the School of Architecture in 2019.

Exhibition example 2

Blue//black the life and legacy of Dr. Carter G. Woodson

Dr. Carter G. Woodson, educator, author, historian, and founder known internationally as the "father of black history," was the second African American to obtain a Ph.D. from Harvard (behind W.E.B. DuBois).[22] Collaborations with UVA's Carter G. Woodson Institute and the Buckingham County African American Historical Society (caretakers of Dr. Woodson's birth site in Buckingham County, New Canton, Virginia) led to the creation of an exhibition titled *blue//black* in fall 2018. Nine students (in three design teams) of the School's Design Thinking curriculum designed *blue//black*, the title referring the blue tones of the nearby James River and the Blue Ridge Mountains, and black, Dr. Woodson's work in African American history and culture.[23]

Stage 1: Empathic discovery

Stage 1 follows Peter Rowe's explication in *Design Thinking*, that "the interior situational logic and decision-making processes of designers in action, as well as the theoretical dimensions that both account for and inform this kind of undertaking."[24] Students (with diverse minors ranging from Social Entrepreneurship to American Studies) collectively practice Rowe's framework, in **strategically created, diverse interdisciplinary design teams** in preparation for initial meetings with members of the Buckingham African American Life and History Society and UVa's Carter G. Woodson Institute. Teams become their own Spiral Group while creating Bearden-influenced collages, visualizing the complex histories of Central Virginia.[25] Shared collages lead feedback discussions on how the region's glorification of plantations and birthplaces for the "founding fathers" in the Central Virginia region compares to the desolate state of Woodson's birth site. Discussions open students to sharing their feelings in these cultural landscapes (Principle 1) and how they are hard to feel into and see themselves within (Principle 2).

In design teams, students begin **empathy training**, reading Dr. Theresa Wiseman's *Concept Analysis of Empathy* and Dr. Helen Reiss' and Gordon Kraft-Todd's *E.M.P.A.T.H.Y. A Tool to Enhance Nonverbal Communication*, in preparation for direct use of learned skills meeting with exhibition stakeholders. Design teams then work through Dorst's **Design Thinking logic** equation, and for student Rohan Kohli, the *WHAT* becoming holding conversations on difficult topics of identity/culture (thinking of Wiseman). *HOW* evolves into creating a "confessional box" (modelled on the religious icon), with challenging questions on race mounted inside, using both articles to test effectiveness with fellow students. For Kohli, *VALUE* becomes developing a space to hear other opinions, without judgment (recalling the Wiseman article, forcing skills of E.M.P.A.T.H.Y.).

Teams learn from Woodson's seminal book *The Mis-Education of the Negro* that cultural indoctrination, instead of teaching, was the experience of African Americans at the time, developing influenced team names (Ground – Up, Mis-Education, and Unwritten). Teams **analyse stakeholders through an empathy lens**, listing potential identities, and individuals who would have slight or no interest in the exhibition with questions similar to those utilized in *Mapping*. Teams return to this list during the semester as an evaluation tool, determining if design ideas create the desired visitor experience from multiple perspectives, and respect Woodson. In design reviews, students adopt these identities for in-class feedback and critiques.

Stage 1 continues as design teams **set goals and objectives** with a "To, By, So That" statement, a professional exhibition design tool from the OSC.[26]

> **To:** (the purpose of our Design is to)
> **By:** (using these *courses of action*)
> **So That:** (how the *courses of action* shift the existing situation to a preferred one)

An example of from design team "Unwritten":

> **To:** Place yourself in a world of complex identities
> **By:** Reflecting on the life and legacy of Dr. Woodson and black culture's role in shaping American history
> **So That:** We are all more informed and aware of the past and ourselves

The **empathy tour** includes a visit to the Birth Site and local community church in New Canton, meeting with leaders from the Buckingham African American Historical Society. The tour puts newly learned empathy skills in action, as students record with Principles 1 and 2 in mind. Students note Principle 1's perspective of Dr. Woodson's life originating at this site in the context of the time, projecting Principle 2's concepts of what forms could be created on the site for *feeling into* historical and community meanings.

Stage 2: Experiential designing and making

Students receive Nuttgens's description, working in design teams while evaluating the *discovery and recognition of needs,* reviewing the archived stakeholder conversations. Alissa Diamond, a Ph.D. student, speaks of the **Identification** of stakeholder needs (and the development of her empathic mindset):

> We prepared for our next community meeting by digging into the stories that the Society had mentioned at the site. From the starting point of one man's life, we began to see a tightly networked set of histories that transcended social, spatial, and temporal scales.

Just from his biography and immediate family history, I saw echoes of all the schoolbook narratives I had learned growing up in Virginia, but from a perspective that had not been given space in my grade school years.[27]

Collection again focuses on Woodson's *The Mis-Education of the Negro*, learning his empathic lens of Design Thinking on African American history and social impact.[28] Inspired by this reading, design teams researched sociocultural precedents following Woodson's inclusive principles, seeking relationships in form. A precedent review includes: evaluating historical content *(how does the design capture sociocultural history, educating the visitor?)*, empathic design composition *(does the design allow for the pragmatic and conceptual definitions of empathy to emerge?)*, and clarity of narrative *(does the design tell this new narrative that could influence sociocultural change?)*. Precedents include the Smithsonian National Museum of African American History and Culture (NMAAHC), Washington, D.C., the National Memorial for Peace and Justice, Montgomery, Alabama, and James Madison's Montpelier's (Mere Distinction of Colour exhibition). The precedent exercise introduces sociocultural design research to students through empathic critical analysis, continuing Rowe's framework, demonstrated in notes from team Ground – Up. Ground – Up details Principles 1 and 2 in action at the National Memorial for Peace and Justice, relating to the empathy articles:

> 800 six-foot body-shaped coffin forms meet visitors around a recognizable agora – like public square (Principle 2) – each etched with names of those lynched in the period of racialized terror in the south. You become face to face with a singular form, connecting to a larger field (and the systematic racial injustices), comprehending the scale of lynching (Principle 1).

Analysis forms in a three-hour studio workshop, developing exhibition Design Briefs, following OSC's Science Content and Design Department examples. Students synthesize learnings, determining content, narrative, visitor experience, exhibition themes, look and feel, and graphic guidelines. The Brief guides the design studio (printed and placed on the common table) for the remainder of the semester, helping students prepare for **Ideation (Prototyping)**, testing exhibition ideas through full-scale foam core mockups, emulating professional exhibition design practice from schematic design to fabrication.

Students begin **Ideation** in the following studio session, visualizing in the first hour, three initial exhibition ideas after reviewing a walkthrough of the NMAAHC (including conversations with students who visited the museum). The second hour includes a visit to empathic exhibitions in the Academical Villages' Rotunda, allowing for an understanding of the full-scale requirements and fabrication required. In the last hour of the studio, students discuss ideas initially in teams, sharing as a group quickly produced exhibition models and sketch drawings. Models and sketches are used to determine the scale of the School of Architecture's exhibition space (dimensions mapped out on the studio's communal table). The **Analysis** studio session guides individual and collective studio work, while continuing to iterate and test ideas – following goals of the Brief while continuing to adopt identities in role-playing scenarios. Next, studio sessions include presenting material options, ensuring content messaging before moving up to foam core mockups at half scale, with each student role-playing with an identity in studio discussions. By result, the **Ideation** stage provides students the rigor required for designing for diverse audiences through a back and forth process of prototyping and identity feedback.

Realization begins in a penultimate review, with full-scale prototypes of foam core. Following the Spiral Group's mindset, reviewers include faculty from departments of Architecture, Medicine, Nursing, Music, and Architectural History, along with stakeholders from the Carter G. Woodson Institute and members of the Historical Society. At the review, students utilize learned empathy skills (from the training) with guests. The effect of the training captures in a Buckingham community member reflecting "how the entry section taught them more about Woodson's life (over what they knew as a lifetime resident educated at Woodson High School." Several guests noted that the confessional booth (designed by student Rohan Kohli) (Figure 2.3) allowed them to discuss racial issues innovatively, creating a conversation mode that simultaneously provided privacy and connectivity. Visitors noticed the nuances in material selection, starting at the beginning of the exhibition with darker tones, progressing to lighter as visitors leave feeling uplifted at the end.

In summary, Historical Society members felt that the exhibition would relate to those interested, and not, in Woodson's life, specifically in student Peyton Spangler's Conversation (Respite) Space (final exhibition shown in Figure 2.2). In this space, visitors could sit on the prized slate (the region's world-famous natural resource) while reading printed copies of Woodson's *Mis-Education*. As the exhibition remained in the School of Architecture, this continually occurred from visitors, leading

Figure 2.2 Final blue//black exhibition, students Megan Hua (Interactive Timeline) photo left, Peyton Spangler (Conversation [Respite] Space) photo right.

to comfortable exchanges and discussions. Following the penultimate review, students refined designs in **Realization**, preparing construction drawings while reviewing with the School's fabrication workshop to ensure constructability. Students completed fabrication in this Stage for display at final reviews with most of the same returning guests in the remaining six weeks of the course.

Stage 3: Empathic implementation

Students' final completed exhibits received extremely positive feedback from stakeholders, faculty, and students, with the *Principles* noted accomplishment throughout the exhibition. Post exhibition feedback noted the embodiment of *Principle 1* – a consistent welcoming sense, and open, comfortable progression of the exhibition thematic and visitor experience. Exhibitions such as Megan Hua's interactive timeline exhibit (Figure 2.2) received extremely positive feedback from *Principle 2*, with each piece of the timeline at a human (hand) scale. In Hua's exhibit, visitors physically investigate African American history, assembling the timeline of Dr. Woodson's life at their own pace while actively participating in Woodson's concept of public history.

The exhibition faces challenges as financial needs are required for future touring beyond the School of Architecture, complicated by the strains and restrictions of the COVID-19 health pandemics. The exhibition is currently in storage, with grant applications in process to facilitate further exposition sites. In light of the current racial justice

Pedagogy + exhibition   49

Figure 2.3 Rohan Kohli (Confession Box – photo left), and Jordan Richardson (Feedback/Question Unit – photo right).

movement, opportunities for a future exhibition are in discussion with the UVa's newly formed *Equity Center, a Democracy Initiative Center for the Redress of Inequity Through Community-Engaged Scholarship.*

Conclusion

Student feedback of the semester was extremely positive, expressing great appreciation for the time allotted to learn empathy skills, directly applying them in collaborations with fellow students, then with invested stakeholders on a real-world project of community importance. Many students stated that the learned skills would be integral in future design studios and professional design aspirations. As an instructor, the levels of supportive collaboration achieved in the semester resulted in a strong level of trust and connective bonds evident in student interactions and in the final exhibition designs. Such faith and bonds allowed for supportive design teams, visitor experience, and progression from beginning to end. Post-graduation, many students continue to correspond to the studio's effects, shaping their professional work in social impact design from locations in North America, India, Japan, and China.

Before each studio class and interaction, self-awareness is critical for the instructor and students – reminding oneself of learned empathy skills, intentions, and growth as the *mosaic* progresses. This emotional preparation, especially in the intensity of our time, must be accounted for and incorporated in studio planning, yet provides deep, community building impacts during the semester. The result is invaluable – with each student achieving their own ethical and aesthetical goals while feeling part of an inclusive unit.

In conclusion, _mpathic design opens students, citizens, organizations, and community members to the skills to devise empathic *courses of action*, not only during their experiential creation on design projects, but throughout the process. The *mosaic* methodology offers a profound human experience by transforming mindsets and cultivating abilities – essential for our divisive climate – as participants understand other perspectives while developing designs. As this chapter demonstrates, the positive effects of the process and resultant outcomes produce empathic design thinkers for the 21st century.

Society member Joe Scruggs of Buckingham summarizes the _mpathic design experience:

> With all of the negative media about the disconnect of young people in today's society and the tensions that exist, as we see our country become more and more polarized, this project was a ray of sunlight and hope, a renewed hope that all is not lost and that these young people are living proof of that hope. We can cross bridges of cultural differences and learn from each other.

Acknowledgements

The collaboration described in this chapter would not be possible without the following: University of Virginia School of Architecture, University of Virginia's Carter G. Woodson Institute, and the Buckingham County African American Life and History Society. I would also like to thank our project advisors: Joyce Gooden, Charles White, Joe Scruggs, Deborah McDowell, Connie Nash, James Perla, Alissa Diamond, Melissa Goldman, and Maurice Wallace. I would also like to thank the students of ARCH 4011, fall 2018, blue//black traveling exhibition Design Thinking Studio: Meg Hua, Cassie Anne Jernigan, Sherina Jhunjhnuwala, Lily Kelly, Rohan Kohli, Bridget Murphy, Jordan Richardson, Peyton Spangler, and Jennifer Tran. I would also like to thank the students of the spring 2018 seminar, as we would not have an exhibition without their exceptional foundation: Emma Hendrix, Andre Johnson, Abigail Ruby Nwaebube, Tehmeena Salahin, Braelyn Schenk, Alison Amos, Elizabeth Ayres, Caroline Bond, Brian

Cameron, Tyler Chartier, Jianna Torre, Elizabeth Zachman, Alissa Diamond, and Graham Fraley. Thank you to Graham Cairns and the team at AMPS (Architecture, Media, Politics, Society) for the opportunity to share this work at the New York (2019) conference.

Notes

1. "Everyday Materials Made Extraordinary: Southern Quilts at BAM," The Seattle Times, accessed May 30, 2020, https://www.seattletimes.com/entertainment/everyday-materials-made-extraordinary-southern-quilts-at-bam/.
2. "One – Way Ticket, Jacob Lawrence Series, Visualizing the Great Migration," Museum of Modern Art, accessed June 10, 2020, https://www.moma.org/interactives/exhibitions/2015/onewayticket/visualizing-the-great-migration/.
3. "Picturing America on Screen," National Endowment for the Humanities, accessed June 8, 2020, https://www.thirteen.org/picturing-america/romare-bearden-the-dove/.
4. "Spiral group," Artsy, accessed June 11, 2020, https://www.artsy.net/gene/spiral-group.
5. "Spiral, Perspectives on African American Art Collective," Studio Museum of Harlem, accessed June 28, 2020, https://studiomuseum.org/exhibition/spiral-perspectives-african-american-art-collective.
6. Recent publications such as Maurie D. McInnis and Louis P. Nelson's Educated by Tyranny and Peter Waldman's Lessons of the Lawn, provide students with this once untold history.
7. Karla McLaren, The Art of Empathy: A Complete Guide to Life's Most Essential Skill. Boulder: Sounds True, 2013 4, 5.
8. John Murray Gibbon, Canadian Mosaic. New York: Dodd, Mead & Company, 1939, 12.
9. "The Lynching of John Henry James," Encyclopedia Virginia, accessed May 24, 2020, https://www.encyclopediavirginia.org/James_The_Lynching_of_John_Henry_1898
10. "Design Thinking," IDEO U, accessed May 9, 2019, https://www.ideou.com/pages/design-thinking
11. Herbert A. Simon, The Sciences of the Artificial. Cambridge, MA: MIT Press, 1996, 111.
12. "Design Thinking and Wicked Problems," Hacker Noon. May 14, 2017. Accessed March 24, 2019. https://hackernoon.com/design-thinking-and-wicked-problems-9265c14fe8e4.
13. Susan Lanzoni, Empathy: A History. New Haven, London: Yale University Press, 2018, 3.
14. Robert Lamb Hart, A New Look at Humanism and "Architectural Empathy: Why Our Brains Experience Places Like People," Metropolis, accessed October 5, 2019, https://www.metropolismag.com/architecture/architectural-empathy-why-our-brains-experience-places-like-people/. Principle 1 also references the work of Craig L. Wilkins, The Aesthetics of Equity: Notes on Race, Space, Architecture, and Music. Minneapolis (USA): University of Minnesota Press, 2007, 3–29.

15. "President's Commission on Slavery and the University," University of Virginia, accessed May 29, 2020, https://slavery.virginia.edu/enslaved-african-americans-at-the-university-of-virginia-walking-tour-map/. The self-guided tour introduces some of the people, places, and stories related to early African American life at the University of Virginia. Between 1817 and 1865, the University relied on the labor of enslaved African Americans, whose presence was undeniably central to the University of Virginia's building and functioning. During the building of the University from 1817 to 1825, dozens of enslaved people yearly labored on nearly all construction aspects. Between 90 and 150 enslaved people lived and worked on Grounds after the University opened its doors to the first session for students in 1825.
16. "The Rotunda," University of Virginia, accessed June 13, 2020, https://rotunda.virginia.edu/lower-east-oval-room.
17. "President's Commission on Slavery and the University, Report to President Teresa A. Sullivan, 2018," University of Virginia, accessed May 22, 2020, https://vpdiversity.virginia.edu/sites/vpdiversity.virginia.edu/files/PCSU%20Report%20FINAL_July%202018.pdf.
18. Riess, Helen, and Gordon Kraft-Todd, "E.M.P.A.T.H.Y." Academic Medicine 89, no. 8 (2014): 1108–112. doi:10.1097/acm.0000000000000287.
19. "President's Commission on Slavery and the University," University of Virginia, accessed May 29, 2020, https://slavery.virginia.edu/rotunda-renovations-complete-new-visitors-center-now-open/.
20. Alan Fletcher, The Art of Looking Sideways. London: Phaidon, 2013, 425–6.
21. Mapping Student Design Team: Siddarth Velamakanni, My – Anh Nguyen, Rosalie Reuss, Michael Tucker, David Reis, Davis Eddy, Arthur Brown, and Hutch Landfair.
22. "Carter G. Woodson." Biography.com. April 16, 2019. Accessed July 05, 2019. https://www.biography.com/scholar/carter-g-woodson.
23. Students of ARCH 4011, fall 2018, blue//black traveling exhibition Design Thinking Studio: Meg Hua – Architecture (BS)/Architectural History (Minor), Cassie Anne Jernigan – Architecture (BS)/Entrepreneurship (Minor), Sherina Jhunjhnuwala – Architecture (BS)/East Asian Studies (Minor), Lily Kelly – Architecture (BS)/Entrepreneurship (Minor), Rohan Kohli – Architecture (BS)/Economics (Minor), Bridget Murphy – Architecture (BS)/Global Sustainability (Minor), Jordan Richardson – Architecture (BS)/Entrepreneurship (Minor), Peyton Spangler – Architecture (BS)/Psychology (Minor), Jennifer Tran – Architecture (BS)/Global Sustainability (Minor)
24. Peter G. Rowe, Design Thinking. Cambridge. MA: MIT Press, 1998, 39–41.
25. Romare Bearden and Harry Henderson, A History of African-American Artists from 1792 to the Present. New York: Pantheon, 1993, 200–14.
26. Process created at the Ontario Science Centre, Science Content and Design Department, Toronto, Ontario, CEO Jennifer Martin, Agents of Change Project Leader, Julie Bowen.
27. Statement provided by ARCH 5500 course student Alissa Diamond.
28. Carter Goodwin Woodson, Mis-Education of the Negro. Wilder Publications, 1977, 144.

3 Pedagogy + intervention
Cumulus, an inhabitable storm

Milagros Zingoni and Magnus Feil

Introduction

Recent studies have recognised the need to develop soft skills during college education regardless of the field of study.[1] Throughout these studies, conducted across the United States and Europe, a series of soft skills have been identified as equally important to the hard skills. They include reliability, risk taking, ability to work under pressure, ability to plan and think strategically, collaboration, communication, creativity, self-confidence, time-management skills, and the willingness to learn and accept responsibility.[2] Across all studies and authors, collaborative skills stood out as a constant. Competence in collaboration is one of the critical abilities that interior architecture (IA) and industrial design (ID) majors are expected to develop during the course of their education.[3] This is in part due to a correlation among collaboration, innovation, and empathic design responses.

Cumulus is the result of a transdisciplinary vertical collaboration between two design studios: one cohort of graduate students in IA, and the other of undergraduate students in ID; both hosted at The Design School at Arizona State University. Together, their studios followed a participatory-design-build pedagogy that applied EDIT, a methodology involving underserved youth from a local Title I K-8 school (Figure 3.1). In the United States, public kindergarten through high schools (K-12) will receive a Title I designation if a minimum of 75% of the student body qualifies for a free or reduced lunch.

Starting with the project's initiation, this chapter follows with a literature review on the topic of design-build studios and on collaboration. Subsequently, it introduces the studio framework, including the participatory collaboration with youth partners from the local Title I school. The study concludes with a discussion of the lessons learned during this collaboration.

DOI: 10.4324/9781003174080-3

54 *Milagros Zingoni and Magnus Feil*

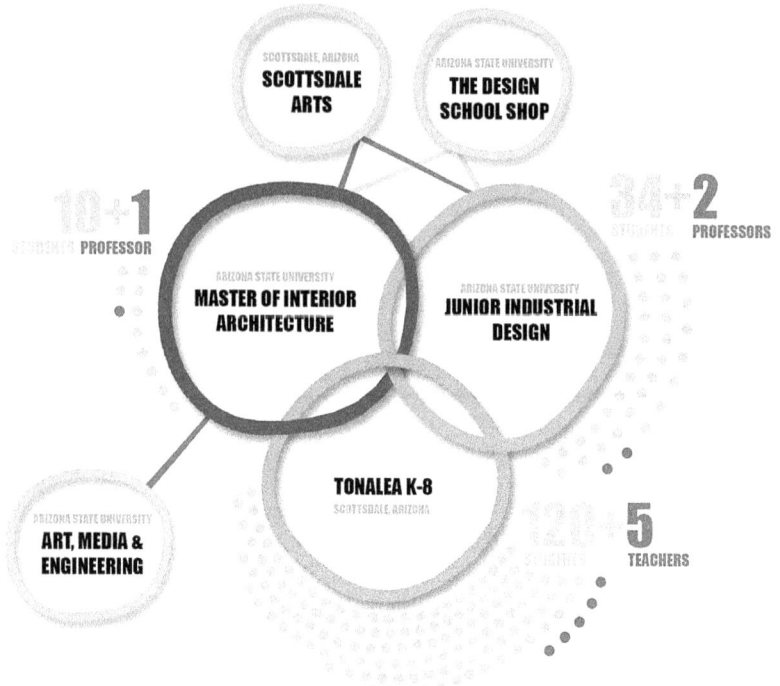

Figure 3.1 Collaboration at multiple scales, Graphic by Ji Hiuk Hong.

Project initiation

Inspired by Mockbee's Rural Studio direction, this project aimed to integrate social and community considerations as a means to temper design students' preconceptions about ID and IA, while encouraging their praxis in an ethical and aesthetic way. This was achieved by including the voices of underrepresented youth (ethics) to enrich the design dialogue while reflecting on students' own practice (aesthetics). The premise of the project entailed teaching the practice of design inclusion to learn design engagement, and to collaborate together with the goal of exposing the youth to social agency. The planning of the collaboration began well before the start of the semester. The faculty requested the K-8 school principal to identify five sixth grade classes that could benefit from this experience.

Strictly contingent upon the interactions with the youth partners, each step of the project was informed by the previous insights gained. The sixth graders participation would inform the design of a temporary installation at the Canal Convergence 2018, a local festival on the waterfront in the downtown area of Scottsdale, Arizona. The project received funding by Scottsdale Arts, a local non-profit organisation sponsored by the city of Scottsdale, Arts Works, the Arizona Commission of the Arts, and the National Endowment for the Arts. While the funding agency met biweekly with the design student for feedback, the design faculty and students had the power to drive the agenda for the project.

Design-build studio

Design studios are student-centred pedagogies applied in design education across all design disciplines including architecture, interior design, ID, landscape architecture, visual communication, IA, and urban design. They involve space and experience in which students learn by doing while solving ill-structured problems.[4] Design studios are collaborative in nature because of "the informality and ephemerality of the way design students communicate and collaborate with each other and the myriad of activities that are social, embodied and experiential in nature."[5]

Design-build studios have been an integral part of architecture education in the United States and across Europe. In the United Kingdom, they are referred as to "live projects," and they include six factors: external collaborator, educational organisation, brief, timescale, budget, and product.[6] In general, they are design studios that produce a full-scale delivery such as a temporary or permanent installation or a building. Design-build studios "can serve as a base for the synthesis, integration, and transformation of knowledge through teaching and project execution."[7] Their pedagogical value has been studied in depth in architecture and landscape architecture. The literature highlights a variety of learning outcomes in this type of studio including integration of previous knowledge of design and construction[8]; becoming better prepared for real professional work[9]; and an increase of confidence.[10] However, in interior design and IA, the concept is slightly shifted to "build to learn" – a pedagogical method that addresses models or full-scale joinery[11] or prefabrication.[12] Moreover, while the concept of design-build studios by itself is relatively unknown by name in ID, the didactic components and outcomes of traditional studio courses closely resemble the "build to learn" approach of interior design. A notable difference, however, is an emphasis on simulating visual appearance, rather than functionality of the designed artefacts.

EDIT studio

EDIT studio adds the first phase to co-create with the youth. It involves engagement, design, implementation, and transformation through the participatory collaboration with partners in the community.[13] The intention behind employing EDIT studio is dualistic: it offers benefits for both design students as well as for the youth involved. On one side, it exposes design students to the development of empathy by working with those with differing realities and a set of experiences other than their own. On the other side, it introduces design thinking and processes, subjects often not taught in K-8 schools. Moreover, it exposes youth to a variety of design disciplines, demystifies preconceived notions about the required skills to be successful in design programmes.[14]

Collaboration in design studios

The term collaboration derives from Latin "co-laborare," which translates to "work with." Collaboration between people, especially in teams, requires communication about intentions, ideas, visions, and knowledge. In design studios, "communication and collaboration between co-designers is multi-modal, multisensory, ubiquitous, and touches the artistic, emotional and experiential side of the designers' thinking, in addition to their instrumental and practical reasoning."[15]

In team-based studios, students develop different collaborative patterns that provide evidence of their ongoing work, allowing them to be in alignment with the project's evolution. This is defined as collaboration awareness. The work produced by students in every iteration, such as sketches, models, and graphics, is known as "coordinative artefacts" and they play an important role in supporting collaboration.[16] In general, scholars identify the importance of the following elements for collaboration within design studios: (1) design studio space, (2) material design artefacts, and (3) bodily conducts (verbal and non-verbal communication).[17] Collaboration between co-designers also plays an important role in creativity.[18] For instance, Engeström[19] argues that the source of creativity is not inside a person's head, but emergent in the interaction between a person's thoughts and their socio-cultural context.

Despite the increased research on collaboration in design studios throughout the last decade, the literature on collaboration in design-build studios is still scarce. It is even more so a reality in transdisciplinary design-build studios. Within the limited literature available for collaboration in design-build education, most articles are written from the faculty's perspective. Such findings include "By working together and with clients, students get an intense exposure to collaboration"[20] and design-build studios contribute to the "development and appreciation of team working skills."[21] In an article written on design-build learning outcomes from the students' perspective, the author quoted the learners in an effort to highlight their perspective on the subject "The lessons we learned about the process of design and working with others will always be with us,"[22] and "I learned that creating in a community and embracing the power of collaboration can be extremely powerful and fulfilling."[23] These students' statements about their design-build experiences create a compelling argument, highlighting the exposure to collaboration throughout design-build education as a venue to learn to work together. In another study on the assessment of cross-disciplinary collaboration outcomes between ID and engineering students, the researchers concluded that "the interdisciplinary teams have produced higher quality results and value both the collaboration as well as the opportunities opened by working with people from another discipline."[24]

Studio framework

The framework of this studio was at the intersection of ethnographic study observations by Vyas et al.[25] that identified three settings within the studio project design process: (1) physical space, (2) artefacts, and (3) verbal and non-verbal communication, and Goff et al., and Visser, and Engestrom's[26] findings on the correlation between creativity and collaboration. Multiple layers of collaboration intended to counteract the prevalent notion that design-build studios hinder creativity due to budget and fabrication constraints. In addition to the collaboration between the students within each studio, and the collaboration across the ID and IA studios, the model also highlighted the collaboration with the youth from the K-8 school. This framework enabled the collaborations across multiple contexts and with multiple specificities under the hypothesis that the creative final product would be associated with the specific collaborative processes (Visser, 2006) and on Engeström's (2001) approach that creativity emerges when ideas are discussed within a social context. In other words, collaboration was used as a strategy to enable creativity, often suppressed in standard approach design-build studios.

This scaffolding placed EDIT methodology, and the subsequent collaborations, at the core of the design process. Similar to the Gestalt theory that states the whole is not simply the sum of its parts, but a synergistic "whole effect,"[27] we explored applying a vertical and transdisciplinary collaboration. The underlying expectation suggested the collective result of the design studios work would produce a stronger result than students' individual efforts and outcomes.

The cumulus project

Due to accreditation standards to which both disciplines were required to adhere, the faculty designed a hybrid learning experience. They ran as one project with two different studios, but interdependent of each other. The IA graduate studio involved 1 faculty and 10 students, and 1 ID undergraduate studio involved 2 faculty and 34 students. The format of the two studios was guided by the Double Diamond Design Process model, and structured into four individual phases: (1) Discovery & Research; (2) Define & Synthesise; (3) Develop & Ideate; and (4) Deliver & Implement,[28] making a strong emphasis on fabrication of tangible prototypes towards full-scale final models.

Both studios had the following outcomes expectations: (1) engagement with youth from a local Title I school, (2) cyclical design iterations responding to the data collected during the interaction with the youth, (3) design development and implementation including construction drawing sets, (4) fabrication, and (5) post-occupation evaluation. Together, both cohorts addressed a coherent identity and the spatial experience throughout the installation and during the production of a final project documentation that described the process in its entirety. The scope of the IA studio addressed a variety of programming such as branding, wayfinding, storytelling, seating, and interaction. The ID studio scope addressed interactions at the scale of the body.

The faculty proposed the project as an ecosystem, a symbiotic relationship in which two or more systems are dependent on each other and which inform each other. In this sense, the faculty used the metaphor of bees and a beehive, in which both elements are dependent on the other one, and without the other part would cease to exist. This concept was carried out through the semester, and ultimately it manifested within the built installation.

The studios were organised into three four-week phases. The first phase was the participatory engagement with the youth, the second phase involved the design of the installation, addressing findings from phase one, and the third phase addressed full-scale fabrication of the final installation. The physical space enabled collaboration and communication.[29] The IA studio was organised with a series of roles. This helped students to develop accountability and ownership towards the project.

Participatory engagement with the youth

The semester launched with a series of games and activities designed to facilitate collaboration and engage different audiences. The intention was to initially expose the college students to similar experiences than those they would be designing themselves to perform with the youth. These undertakings would also become the foundation for the first set of activities with the 120 sixth graders. A partner from Rohd's Theater Company curated this first set of ice breaker activities with the ID and IA students. These activities followed Rohd's (1998) book, *Theater for Community, Conflict and Dialogue*.[30]

The design students designed, tested, and executed the five visits to the local K-8 school engaging five sixth grade teachers and their students. The first visit involved all 120 students gathered at the cafeteria where they participated in the ice-breaking games. Through these activities, they shared early on experiences and values in a variety of educational settings around the topic of "community and its relationship with water." The overall aim of the games was to engage the youth in the design process and facilitate a user-centred approach with the ID and IA students. "Framing collaborative design activities in a game format arguably improves idea-generation."[31]

As previously mentioned, all design students participated in these activities introduced in Rohd's book during their first day of their own semester. These warm-up exercises and bridging activities started with "Thumbs Up," an initial game that helped to build excitement for subsequent planned activities. This game challenged the youth to stimulate an awareness of each other both during the game and for the rest of the day. Subsequent activities included: (1) "circle dash,"[32] a game with the objective of finding someone else to switch places by using silent signals while preventing others from learning their plan to switch; (2) "cover the space,"[33] a game with the intention of getting people up and involved in the least threatening way (Figure 3.2D); (3) "fill in the blank," an activity that asks participants to complete sentences given by the moderators in flashcards; and (4) "organising by birthdays" a task to create one large circle with all participants organised by birthdates by only using non-verbal communication. Parallel to exercise (4), selected design students organised and processed the data collected from the flashcards in the previous games (1–3). Still, in the birthdate circle, the AI students read aloud the data collected from

Figure 3.2 (A) Interior architecture graduate students testing the "headbands exercise." (B) sixth to eighth graders making headdresses that represent their community. (C) Fill in the blanks "What are the things you value the most about your community and how it relates to the value of water in the context of the desert?." (D) sixth to eighth graders making their infrastructures close to the water for their communities. Image 4 shows the 4As exercise being used as a reference when designing. (E) Youth recreating a storm sound through a variety of materials.

the groups and asked the youth to raise their hand upon hearing their answers. These semi-structured interviews, answers, and this final activity found commonalities among the youth, their teachers, the university students, and their faculty. These planned activities were not random; they constituted building blocks that allowed the team to develop future in-class activities.[34] They also enabled the group "to play in a safe space, and to create a sense of comfort in the collective doing of specific and structured activities,"[35] while generating initial data sets.

One of the rules set by the design faculty determined that all activities planned for the middle schoolers should first be prototyped, experienced, and tested by the design students themselves (Figure 3.2A). Each set of questions required a specific subset of activities. For instance, during the second visit, the graduate students led a "headband workshop" using recycled materials only. They tasked the youth to design, describe, and wear a headband to represent their community. As a result, 116 unique designs were collected with corresponding reflections from the youth's voices (Figure 3.2B). During the third visit, a series of "fill in the blank" sheets were created and distributed. The underlying rationale of this exercise involved encouraging in-depth reflection about the youth's values towards their community and the meaning of water in the context of desert cities (Figure 3.2C). Over the course of the fourth visit, design students introduced an exercise called "4 As" with the purpose of introducing the youth to the generation of a programme for infrastructures next to water canals in their community. A brief lecture introduced this ethnographic study that asked the youth to identify all (1) actors, (2) activities, (3) artefacts, and (4) atmospheres involved in the installations they envisioned. The actors represent the people that would use this installation, what activities they imagine these actors would accomplish in the space, and what artefacts would facilitate such activities. The atmospheres would be created as a result of the actors performing those activities with those artefacts. Using cardstock, students subsequently designed and prototyped their ideal spaces inspired by their 4As analysis (Figure 3.2D). These large sets of collaborative methods and approaches that designers employ in their design activities are defined by Vyas et al. (2013) as creative social practices. These three visits defined the scope and the parti (poetics and inception) of the project for the design students.

Through data analysis of these first three exercises, a commonality emerged highlighting the youth's values that: (1) they were all individual pieces of a larger system, (2) this system was interdependent, and (3) that this represents a big puzzle, of which their community is comprised. A uniting perception around the notion of water was how "they all loved the monsoons, a typical storm of the desert. The excitement and anticipation of the storm and the disappointment that their parents don't let them play during the storm and instead they have to see it through a window of their homes." Across their 4As exercise recurring values included: a place to chill, a place to belong, a place to be with friends, and a system of proverbial "secret buttons," akin to a magic wand, that would trigger specific actions or commands. These findings provided meaning and direction to the design students: design an "inhabitable storm."

Based on the value of drawing as a strong means of communication in design disciplines, the fourth visit involved several collaborative drawing exercises in which a portion of the illustration was started by one student, then followed by a multitude of classmates. The final results only became visible at the end of the exercise. This element of surprise not only proved entertaining, it also delivered powerful insights and something new that is unique to design education: creating a temporal dissection of unfolding events through storytelling. The fifth and final visit to the K-8 school offered an immersive and interactive experience: music. To help visualise the inhabitable storm, the ID students prepared discovery tools for making weather sounds (Figure 3.2E) and the classes performed a weather system with the help of simple props.

A visit to the university campus concluded the official collaboration portion of the project. The 120 sixth graders visited The Design School to learn firsthand about the design and fabrication of the installation informed by the previous activities with them. The youth witnessed the fabrication in progress, experienced the ID and IA physical studio settings, and visited different campus fabrication facilities, such as the wood shop, the digital lab, and the "maker space." The visit supported the organiser's original intent of exposing underrepresented youth in design to the fields of ID and IA. Moreover, it aimed to encourage the sixth graders to act as ambassadors of the project during the upcoming ten days of public display at the Scottsdale's Canal Convergence Festival.

Implementing insights: Design informed by youth participation

The implementation of insights was not a synchronous process. In a way, information flowed at a steady rate. This transpired in between the two studios and the piece-by-piece together of the youth. The parti of an inhabitable storm combined with the atmospheres the youth sought within the public realm, materialised through three elements: (1) a *cloud*, (2) four *windows with benches* representing the inside of a living room (to watch the storm), and (3) 15 individual *drops* as the proverbial molecules of a storm. By itself, this created a cloud of opportunities.

IA students developed the idea of the cloud as the central element of the installation, the windows with benches as the components that would frame the cloud and drops – while ID students took ownership of the drops as 15 smaller interactive installations (Figure 3.3). Each of the drops offered an immersive experience by touching on one or more senses closely associated with the passing of a monsoon. Some of the strategies deployed included the use of light, sound, smell, and other elements of discovery, such as temporal experiences. Examples of "drops" are: (1) a station that emitted the smell of creosote bushes, a local phenomenon that only occurs after rainfall; (2) an installation

Figure 3.3 CUMULUS Installation at Canal Convergence: a cloud, the drops and the windows with benches of the living room.

of two facing seats, one featuring a button to trigger a flash of light, the other receiving vibration after an interval of time, aimed to display the relationship between lightning and thunder; and (3) a third installation played with the element of surprise by creating a dialogue between two components: an umbrella and a cloud, each featuring a pull string. Once pulled, the cloud would light up, while the umbrella would start raining onto the visitor.

The *cloud* offered an interactive experience triggered by embedded motion sensors that mimicked a spectrum of light and colours depending on the visitor's movement and interactions. It also showcased our partnering youth's values and reflections about community and water. The back of the cloud served as a video projection space featuring storytelling about the entire design collaboration process from ideation to implementation. The *living room windows with benches* framed the *cloud* and the *drops* helping to define the space. They also offered an opportunity to sit and stay, showcased the shared value of the ID and IA students, and, most importantly, curated the sixth graders' drawings and models.

Studio culture

Both physical studios had high visual and material character as they were filled with materials, models, full-scale prototypes for ergonomic purposes, electronic prototypes to ensure functionality, and full-scale models of joinery to develop details and fabrication techniques.

The studio walls showcased the work produced in collaboration with the youth, data analysis and programming diagrams, post-its and notes regarding the scope and intention of the project, sketches, photos of the site, materials, and inspirations. The public availability and shared knowledge of these artefacts helped support the communication and coordination among the design teams,[36] and enabled students to challenge and inspire new ideas, to create cross-contextual reminders that lead to breakthrough thinking and conceptualisation.[37]

Throughout the design development, students tracked the progress of design evolution.[38] This "ecological richness of design studios stimulates creativity in a manner that is useful and relevant to the ongoing design tasks"[39] and so does the constant practice of interim reviews, to show others the work in progress in search for feedback to inform the next iteration. This is referred to by Schön[40] as the reflective practice of the designer that encourages discourse and reflection during the design process. The fieldwork on designers by Vyas et al. underscores the centrality of "thinking through doing" (or thinking through externalising) together collectively developing an average of 50–100 external representations of their design ideas. This manifested in both IA and ID studios across multiple team sizes.

Discussion and challenges

As university classes need to adhere to accreditation standards, the first challenge of this project for the involved faculty was to comply with them. Despite this challenge, the partnership between the faculty and their studios proved to be an effective way to deconstruct the ivory towers of the design domains, while breaking the invisible silos that still largely rule and divide design disciplines. Thanks to the carefully crafted faculty planning and the support of the K-8 school principal, the underlying collaboration with the youth went exceptionally well. The sixth graders looked forward every week to the experience of working with the university students on design thinking.

The varying class sizes directly influenced a different set of challenges: for the ten-student IA studio, working together towards a shared vision proved difficult. Finding consensus among students required individuals to subordinate more towards shared ideas and goals. Students had to be educated to shift the dialogue from an egocentric "my idea" to the direction of rescinding individual ownership for a group-driven common goal. Another challenge associated with a group of ten working on one project was the individual accountability and the amount of time invested into the studio project. On the other hand, the much larger class size of the ID cohort tasked the instructors to manage a total of 15 unique projects with individual challenges. At the same time, the multiple levels of complexity associated with the different components of the installation, forced students to consistently look inward to develop their emerging individual concepts in context with the work of others, and the cumulus ecosystem in general (outward).

In design, intangible ideas soon take on physical shape. To accomplish this, some students improved their use of machinery skills along the fabrication process. The experimentation with different materials, processes, and sketches, also enabled a quick generation of ideas. For instance, the "interactive cloud" went through a series of technological iterations besides the ones related to form. These technological iterations addressed how to activate light through different modes of human interaction: movement, touch, pressure, etc. Earlier iterations proposed the interactive component by completing the electrical circuit with the body. Additionally, both ID and IA students struggled with the adaptation of new technologies to facilitate interactivity. For instance, some designs required mechanical and electrical components involving soldering, Arduino coding, and special fabrication of pieces to control components. The skills obtained were directly proportionate to the number of hours that each student devoted to the (work) shop. Furthermore, the nature of fabrication necessitated close collaboration among students. The carefully crafted timeline became negatively impacted by the less committed individuals, resulting in additional workload for others. This issue arose again during the end of the semester student peer- and self-evaluations. Here, some expressed that despite a love for the project overall and the considerable skills acquired, students contended there was a perceivable discrepancy between the time invested by the most committed team members and peers with lower investment.

Unlike traditional studio projects, design-builds offer the ability to test practical solutions, such as structures, durability, and safety. In this particular project, public engagement during the ten-day event allowed faculty and students to test the design intentions beyond the tangible aspects.

Conclusions

This study proposed that different design discipline studios can work together, exploring the intersection between them to improve creativity while engaging voices often unheard (youth) to explore design as a social agency. The outcomes underscored that by working across design disciplines and with multiple audiences (youth, undergraduate, and graduate design students), it is possible to develop stronger collaborative skills at multiple levels and improve the creative outcomes. Moreover, working with youth to empower them as community agents throughout the ideation process proved critical to the project mission. Yet, pending studies are the impact (if any) for the youth involved in the project, and the conflicts in collaboration when not all students are equally invested in the project.

The process of making, the better understanding of the youth's shared values, the transdisciplinary set of students and faculty eager to expand design-build education, infused deeper meaning to the process for everyone involved. Ultimately, the same metaphor used to describe the collaboration between the studios as "the beehive and the bees" early in the semester, was reflected in the poetics of the "Cumulus" installation. Together, the ID and IA students developed an interdependent experience in which each piece relies upon another one to co-exist. The multiple collaboration formats enriched the design learning experience. In these varied collaborations, verbal and non-verbal communications were pivotal to share and find consensus about the design ideas and common goals but also in order to align the team. Overall, the physical spaces of the two studios seemed to enable good collaboration. However, the faculty believes that the collaboration could have been enhanced if both studios were to share the same physical space.

Working as a large team with smaller subgroups, forced students to create more than one proposal to the same core idea, and helped to develop collaborative skills while increasing creativity. Throughout the design process, it seems that quick models were easier for collaboration and dialogue. The three-dimensional models allowed the teams to discuss the design evolution by quickly modifying the models with tape or breaking them apart to develop the idea into a new quick model. These quick models encouraged discussions and new iterations in contrast with progress renderings that were perceived as finalised ideas. This supports the argument by Vyas et al. that "thinking through doing" suggests the effort invested in developing different design alternatives helps co-designers to compare and judge important aspects and overcome challenges such as the difficulty of fabricating the final product.

The collaboration with the 120 students from the local school helped the design students develop a sense of ethics and responsibility towards projecting the voices of the middle schoolers. On this note, the project avoided being a stereotypical "helicopter project" in which university students predominantly focus on the outcome rather than the process and the social responsibility of the project. The fact that design students and faculty were able to recognise their youth partners among a crowd of 200,000 visitors during the ten-day long festival is a testament to that commitment. In other words, this project created the sensibility for design students to care and find a deeper meaning in their creations to reflect the youth's values. Additionally, it permitted exposure to the shifting or broadening of the scope of design, from consumption to design for agency. This is a virtue that needs to be instilled in future designers. Maybe the path to achieving this is by including design as a social agency within tomorrow's accreditation standards. Moreover, the installation was funded by the city for a local event, which enabled design students to develop a sense of responsibility towards the timeline for product delivery and financial responsibility. In design-build-funded studios, there is no room for failure since there is an expectation for product delivery and therefore the latter can constrain creativity in design students. Yet, in this case, creativity was mainly developed and enhanced as a result of the collaborations across multiple contexts and scales and through the playful and informed collaboration with youth.

Most design students who currently seek design-build opportunities, transdisciplinary collaborations, and service-learning experiences, are unaware that this type of project requires more time than traditional studios. In an era where the number of non-traditional students is increasing, not all students are able to commit to the (at times, significant) extra time needed. Therefore, design-build studios should be elective instead of required. This type of studio also requires more time on behalf of the faculty, and they need to be made aware that the stakes are much higher than traditional studios. For instance, faculty must address a studio culture that considers all potential challenges in collaboration including systems to enable collaboration, systems to monitor consistency and accountability, and resiliency as a response to multiple design changes and fabrication processes.

EDIT design-build studios provide students with the opportunity of developing an ethical responsibility to the community partners (in this case, the sixth graders), developing their divergent thinking by exploring a variety of ideas that represents the shared values of the partners, developing convergent thinking by fabricating the full-scale installations, increasing their creative problem-solving abilities, and enabling them to develop a wide range of soft skills, with measurable impact. Notwithstanding, working collaboratively and holistically throughout a participatory-transdisciplinary design-build project, enabled students to create a better understanding of each other, the community, and the power of design in general.

Acknowledgements

This chapter would have not been possible without the collaborators that we have worked with along the way. Special thanks to our funding agency: Scottsdale Public Art and Scottsdale Arts: Natalie Marsh & Staff, and to our supportive industry partners: Airpark Signs & Graphics and The Walter Hive; to The Design School Shop – Jesus Orozco, Ben Bednarz, Mark Fromeyer, & Julian Silva, and to the ASU Library Makerspace. They all gave their time and expertise to guide the students with such care.

A special thanks to the students we have worked with. They make our work on these projects an absolute joy; and their talent and creative thinking is certainly something worth shouting about: Arizona State University – Fall 2018 – Advanced Studio Interior Architecture: Shahrina Afrin + Amanda Ahlman + Dania Alarfaj + Susan Clay + Rachel Frail + Ji Hyuk Hong + Adetoniola Osarieme Rebecca Makinde + Kara Moncada + Neha Vikas Tendulkar + Zijing Zhao.

Industrial Design Studio III: Joseph Avrett + Michelle Bocanegra Batriz + Ruben Campos + Jane Chen + Maddy Cika + Solomon Conway-Janes + Luca De Simone + Austin Dell + Huiying Fang + Yifan Fang + Carley Fortier + Nico Francis + Cole Frederick + Ruoying Ge + Cindy Eunsoo Kim + Jeannie Kozicki + Becca Leonard + Catharine Lewis + Binghui Li + Rachel Tingyu Lin + Zihao Liu + Sijie Ma + Erlend Meling + Cooper Newnam + Becca Oberrieder + Henry Ripley + Marco Rufeo + Shirly Tam + Yuna Song + Emily Terpstra + Jennifer Torloni + Liang Wang + Joshua Weinstein + Chace Younger + Stephanie Hui Zhang.

To the new generation of designers: our sixth graders, their teachers, and their Principal Dr. Priniski from Tonalea K-8 School: Ms. Campini + Abigail A. + Magdalena A. + Christopher A. + Sally B. + Thomas B. + Ehmann C. + Abigail D. + Jacob D. + Achilles E. + James H. + Andrew H. + Haley H. + Jennifer I. + Leonardo L. + Dominic M. + Luis M. + Kimberly M. + Ricky M. + Jaymie N. + Evelyn O. + Elena P. + Cody R. + Giselle R. + Jayden S. + Guadalupe T. + Sierra T. + Juan V. + Justin W. + Alina W. + Savina W. + Kayla W. + Tyre W. + Jonah Z. Ms. Lucero + Diana A. + Natalee A. + Rosanna B. + Alejandra

B. + Angel C. + Carmen D. + Estela E. + Alejandro F. + Jonathan G. + Andres H. + Giabella J. + James L. + Mia L. + Kimberly L. + Linda L. + Travis M. + Daisy M. + Yeshua M. + Katteryn M. + Jalen P. + Leilani P. + Sofia P. + Kailana R. + Zabdiel V. + Jacob W. + Connor W. + Kayla W. Ms. Merrick + Derek A. + Jesus A. + Bianca A. + Eljin B. + Daisy B. + Angel C. + Zaydrie C. + Mikhail D. + Hailey D. + Ali E. + Genesis G. + Jaqueline G. + Emili G. + Vanessa G. + Jordy H. + Alexander I. + Mark O. + Zayuri O. + Robert P. + Wayde Q. + Reagan R. + Jacob R. + Amarye R. + Marandy S. + Emily S. + Andy T. + Savina W. + Isabella Z. Ms. Slamowitz + Angel A. + Jazmyn B. + Christian C. + Jason D. + Ava F. + Heidi F. + Hector G. + Itzel G. + Dafney H. + Dominic J. + Masen K. + Brayan L. + Matthew M. + Noel M. + Reina M. + Marisol Q. + Jaden R. + Yanire S. + Valerie S. + Tre T. Ms. Solberg + Nathaniel A. + Gabrielle A. + Cassandra C. + Samantha D. + Abigail D. + Jacob D. + Samuel F. + Joshua G. + Anthony G. + Jennifer I + Aleena J. + Aidan M. + Jenny M. + Cyndi M. + Luis M. + Jaymie N. + Elena P. + Melanie R. + Jiselle R. + Riddeck R. + Cody R. + Giselle R. + Oscar S. + Diego S. + Brian S. + Luke T. + Brandon W. + Aiden W. + Justin W. + Kayla W. + Jonah Z.

Finally, our gratitude to Professor Graham Cairns and the team at Amps who have provided us with the opportunity to present this collaboration along the way in their conference in New York (2019), and for connecting us with Laura Sanderson + Sally Stone who made this book possible. It has been a joyful and rewarding ride.

Notes

1. Davidson, Cathy N. *The New Education: How to Revolutionize the University to Prepare Students for a World in Flux.* New York: Basic Books, 2017.
2. Elias, Peter, and Kate Purcell. "Is Mass Higher Education Working? Evidence from the Labour Market Experiences of Recent Graduates." *National Institute Economic Review*, no. 190 (2004): 60–74.
3. Vyas, Dhaval, Heylen, Dirk and Nijholt, Anton. "Creative Practices in the Design Studio Culture: Collaboration and Communication." *Cognition, Technology and Work*, no. 1 (2013): 425–443.
4. Schön, D. A. (1982). *The Reflective Practitioner: How Professionals Think in Action.* Basic Books Inc., New York.
5. Vyas, Dhaval, Heylen, Dirk and Nijholt, Anton. "Creative practices in the design studio culture: Collaboration and communication." *Cognition, Technology and Work* (2013): p. 415.
6. Chad, K. (2017) *Design Build Education.* Routledge. Taylor and Francis Group, New York and London, 2017.

7. Hinson, David, "Design as Research: Learning from Doing in the Design-Build Studio." *Journal of Architectural Education* 61, no. 1 (2007): 23–26, 23.
8. Luescher, Andreas. "Concrete Geometry: Playing with Blocks." *International Journal of Art & Design Education* 29, no. 1 (2010): 17–26.
9. Winterbottom, Daniel. "Building to Learn, Part II: Reflections on a Decade of Developing a Design Build Program [University of Washington, Seattle]." *Landscape Architecture* 93, no. 4 (2003): 72.
10. Badanes, Steve. The Architect as Builder: The case for design/build. In W. Carpenter (Ed.), *DBS: Design Build Studio*. Decatur, GA: Lightroom Studios, 2010, pp. 84–87.
11. Konkel, Margaret T. "Build-to-Learn: An Examination of Pedagogical Practices in Interior Design Education." *Journal of Interior Design* 39, no. 2 (2014): 1–16.
12. Schneiderman, Deborah. "The Prefabricated Interior: Defining the Topic." *Interiors 2*, no. 2 (July 2011): 189–211.
13. Zingoni, Milagros. EDIT STUDIO 1.0: A Practiced Oriented Design Studio using Collaborative Process to Engage the community, Define a problem, Infer solutions, to socially embed Transformation. EDULEARN 2014 International Conference, Barcelona, Spain (2014): 6822–6829.
14. Zingoni, Milagros. Leveraging design education to empower youth to be agents of change in their community. In conference Proceedings Great Asian Streets Symposium/Pacific Rim Community Design Network/Structures for Inclusion Singapore (2018): 457–467.
15. Vyas, Dhaval, Heylen, Dirk and Nijholt, Anton. "Creative Practices in the Design Studio Culture: Collaboration and Communication." *Cognition, Technology and Work*, no. 1 (2013): 425–443, 416.
16. Schmidt, Kjeld and Wagner, Ina. Coordinative artefacts in architectural practice. In M. Blay-Fornarino et al. (Eds.), *Proceedings of the Fifth International Conference on the Design of Cooperative Systems (COOP 2002)*. Amsterdam: IOS Press, 2002, pp. 257–274.
17. Vyas, D., Heylen, D. and Nijholt, A. Physicality and cooperative design. In Proceedings of the 5th joint workshop on machine learning and multimodal interaction (MLMI' 08). Lecture Notes in Computer Science, Springer, Berlin (2008), pp. 325–337.
18. Vyas, Dhaval, Heylen, Dirk and Nijholt, Anton. "Creative Practices in the Design Studio Culture: Collaboration and Communication." *Cognition, Technology and Work* (2012): 1–29.
19. Yrjö Engeström. "Expansive Learning at Work: Toward an Activity Theoretical Reconceptualization." *Journal of Education and Work* 14, no. 1 (2001): 133–156. DOI: 10.1080/13639080020028747.
20. Melcher, Katherine. "Leaving the Drafting Table: Students' Perspectives on the Design-Build Experiences." *Landscape Research Record* 1, (2013): 72–82. 77.
21. Wallis, L. Building the Studio Environment. In Ashraf M. Salama and N. Wilkinson (Eds.), *Design Studio Pedagogy*. Gateshead, UK: Urban International Press, 2007, pp. 201–208, 208.
22. Reker, J. L. "Design/Build: Real Life Education." *Crit*, no. 31 (1993): 28–32, 32.

23. Kleman, J. qtd. in Tygart, J. Drury University design-build program. In W. Carpenter (Ed.), *DBS: Design Build Studio*. Decatur, GA: Lightroom Studio, 2010, pp. 152–155.
24. Goff, R., Terpenny, Janis, Vernon, Mitzi and Green, W. R. Evolution of student perception in a Human Centered Interdisciplinary Design Project. Proceedings – Frontiers in Education Conference (2006): 7. DOI: 10.1109/FIE.2006.322586.
25. Vyas, Dhaval, Heylen, Dirk and Nijholt, Anton. Creative Practices in the Design Studio Culture: Collaboration and Communication. *Cognition, Technology and Work*, no. 1 (2013), 425–443.
26. Visser, Willemien. *The Cognitive Artifacts of Designing*. Mahwah, NJ: L. Erlbaum Associates, 2006. Yrjö Engeström. "Expansive Learning at Work: Toward an Activity Theoretical Reconceptualization." *Journal of Education and Work* 14, no. 1 (2001), 26, 133–156. DOI: 10.1080/13639080020028747.
27. Behrens, Roy. "Art, Design and Gestalt Theory." *Leonardo* 31, no. 4 (1998): 299–303.
28. Nessler D. (2016). How to apply a design thinking, HCD, UX or any creative process from scratch [Online]. Available at: https://medium.com/digital-experience-design/ how-to-apply-a-design-thinking-hcd-ux-or-any-creative-process-from-scratchb8786eff812 [Accessed 12 Mar. 19].
29. Vyas, Dhaval, Heylen, Dirk and Nijholt, Anton. "Creative Practices in the Design Studio Culture: Collaboration and Communication." *Cognition, Technology and Work*, no. 1 (2013): 425–443.
30. Rohd, Michael. *Theatre for Community, Conflict & Dialogue: The Hope Is Vital Training Manual*. Portsmouth, NH: Heinemann, 1998.
31. Eva Brandt, Jörn Messeter, Facilitating collaboration through design games, Proceedings of the Eighth Conference on Participatory Design: Artful Integration: Interweaving Media, Materials and Practices, July 27–31, 2004, Toronto, Ontario, Canada. p. 121.
32. Rohd, Michael. *Theatre for Community, Conflict & Dialogue: The Hope Is Vital Training Manual*. Portsmouth, NH: Heinemann, 1998. p. 10.
33. Rohd, Michael. *Theatre for Community, Conflict & Dialogue: The Hope Is Vital Training Manual*. Portsmouth, NH: Heinemann, 1998. p. 12.
34. Zingoni, Milagros. Leveraging design education to empower youth to be agents of change in their community. In Conference Proceedings Great Asian Streets Symposium/Pacific Rim Community Design Network/Structures for Inclusion Singapore (2018): 457–467.
35. Rohd, Michael. *Theatre for Community, Conflict & Dialogue: The Hope Is Vital Training Manual*. Portsmouth, NH: Heinemann, 1998. p. 4.
36. Perry, Mark and Sanderson, Duncan. "Coordinating Joint Design Work: The Role of Communication and Artefacts." *Design Studies* 19, no. 3 (1998): 273–288.
37. Eli Blevis, Lim, Youn-kyung, Stolterman, Erik, Wolf, Tracee Vetting and Sato, Keichi. Supporting design studio culture in HCI. In CHI '07 Extended abstracts on human factors in computing systems (CHI '07). New York, NY: ACM. (2007): 2821–2824.
38. Sachs, Avigail. "'Stuckness' in the Design Studio." *Design Studies* 20, no. 2 (1999): 195–209.

39. Vyas, Dhaval, Heylen, Dirk and Nijholt, Anton. "Creative practices in the design studio culture: Collaboration and communication." *Cognition, Technology and Work*, no. 1 (2013): 425–443, 415.
40. Schön, Donald A. *The Reflective Practitioner: How Professionals Think in Action.* New York, NY: Basic Books, 1983.

4 Pedagogy + production space
Steam & the city

Alessandro Columbano

Introduction

Birmingham, in the West Midlands, is the largest city in the United Kingdom outside of London. Its heritage as a 19th-century industrial city is still ever present in its culture and the creative sectors it hosts in the region. However, there are three conditions that are affecting the relationship between the city, its creative industry, and the economic impact it generates.

It has one of the strongest manufacturing profiles in the country[1] but the sector is competing with the city's strong service economy and a burgeoning creative industry. Artists and creatives are moving to the region in high numbers as they are being priced out of the South-East, but with limited cultural infrastructures to support them in order to develop their practice.

In parallel to this demographic dynamic, state education is making changes to national policy, with the Design Council highlighting how these will affect employment in the creative sector as there is a sharp drop in design degrees.[2] As a result, Higher Education (HE) is looking at new initiatives to take a share in the competitive University market, to attract more students, and to bring in more investment through research and enterprise. In this context, Birmingham City University (BCU), a former vocational polytechnic turned University, has the largest art and design HE faculty outside of London.

As a counter to these effects in internal displacement and state education, BCU has established STEAMhouse, a centre for creative innovation and physical prototyping with a STEAM design philosophy for small- and medium-sized enterprises (SMEs) to develop new products and for designers/artists to further develop their practice. It offers a support network for graduates during setting up new enterprises and is fostering a creative community that in turn will attract more talent to the region.

DOI: 10.4324/9781003174080-4

74 *Alessandro Columbano*

This chapter will explore the impact of STEAMhouse against the marketisation of education while drawing parallels to the city's industrial heritage and how its historic development has helped define the programme and building. It will highlight the collaborative network it required, combining academics working with artists and designers to create a support network for the community, and demonstrate how the institution worked within more fluid processes of smaller organisations to establish STEAMhouse in the city.

STEAM education as a political response

STEAM is an educational approach that integrates the arts with "STEM" subjects (science, technology, engineering, and mathematics) to enable developments in critical thinking and creative exploration that can be applied to global challenges. It is cited that the abbreviated term was first coined by Harvey White, co-founder of a telecoms company at a San Diego Economic Development forum stating, "we simply cannot compete in the new economy unless we do something now about creativity and innovation."[3]

What started as a discussion on embedding creative practice in industry, STEAM has gained traction as an educational method, predominantly in Further and Higher Education Institutions (HEIs) in North America (Rhode Island School of Design, RISD initiated the design approach) and more recently in institutions in the United Kingdom.

RISD's documentation in setting up a STEAM educational initiative is described in their online Catalogue 1. It established a STEAM ecosystem gaining momentum at the height of the last recession – as a form of a political reaction, furthering the role of Universities to include a civic responsibility at a time the public sector was restricted in providing a place for the arts in society. The Catalogue describes the realisation of "one of the values that art and design can bring to a multidisciplinary process was the ability to extort 'happy accidents' ... a number of the projects resulted from something accidental being turned up to a higher level."[4]

Nesta, the UK Innovation Foundation, has begun to document how STEAM subjects have been taken up in the national curriculum as well as by the University groups and one of their reports has attempted to visualise STEAM subjects at secondary/college level in Scotland. The broader landscape paints a bleak picture where the uptake of the arts subjects is in decline and 50% of schools have closed down art and design departments since 2000.[5] This trend is counterintuitive to the recent success of the creative economy in the United Kingdom – the Department for Culture, Media and Sports reports a 50% increase in UK gross value added (GVA) for the creative industry between 2010 and 2017.[6] Therefore, what will happen to the future pipeline for the design industry and creative arts? The University sector is preparing for the impact of national policy on the state curriculum in the arts by developing new routes into education and nurturing a talent pool through an increase in apprenticeships, emerging subject areas, establishing foundation courses, and coordinating public activities or school engagement programmes.

STEAM in the local context

In the United Kingdom, the makerspace landscape has been mapped by Nesta. In detailing the spaces' aspirations, their qualitative research indicates the plugging of gaps that have been omitted by both the public and private sectors. They "look out to their local community, or aim to tackle specific local issues, such as developing a rural economy, addressing unemployment, or providing an alternative to school–based education ... development is a primary ambition for most makerspaces ... makerspaces often try to support members in completing challenging projects or developing their own businesses."[7]

In the case of Birmingham, a STEAM approach was developed as a response to specific circumstances in its social, cultural, and political context of the city, established by two key players: The Birmingham School of Architecture and Design (BSoAD, a department within BCU) and Eastside Projects (EP) – an internationally respected artist-led gallery. This chapter will document the circumstances for these "supporters" of the idea to interpret and implements a STEAM design approach. It is applied to the context of Birmingham's creative scene and manufacturing sector with the establishment of STEAMhouse, an innovation and prototyping centre housed within a 1500 sqm building in Digbeth, the industrial heartland of Birmingham. (Figure 4.1).

Supporters for a space for production

Before the building was established, STEAMhouse was conceived as a different type of makerspace in its planning phase, with a relationship grown from individual acquaintances between the two core organisations (BCU and EP), including the author of this chapter. We became "supporters" in establishing a production space for graduates, artists, and makers to create a studio environment where innovative new

76 Alessandro Columbano

Figure 4.1 A range of workspaces available for members in STEAMhouse.

artistic practices could emerge. The term "supporters" is used in reference to the supporters on either side of the Birmingham Coat of Arms – an artist and an engineer, providing both the city's identity and prosperity through its industry.

The author, from the BSoAD, wanted to develop a fabrication facility to test and build large structures for live projects, experimental material processes and to encourage graduates to stay in the city as a result of potential creative opportunities. Similarly, Ruth Claxton, artist and Associate Director at EP, wanted to provide opportunities for creatives to further their own work and nurture local talent to improve their artistic development beyond what the current ecosystem could provide.

As an arts organisation, EP describes itself as an artist-run multiverse. In 2013, they published the 6th edition of their user manual, showing how their creative organisation runs (and some of the ideas behind them) with artists Peter Nencini and James Langdon interpreting the supporters of Birmingham on the city's historic coat of arms, as a layered urban landscape to question the role of the artist in all the city's development.

There is a suggestion that an organisation such as EP acts as (or become) the cultural engineers needed to produce a facility like STEAMhouse, as they understand what is needed in the community. In many of EP's shows, their vision as a gallery for the public is also to question the role of a gallery in forging a new city and reclaiming Birmingham as a place of production – as exemplified by Production Show; a two-year series of exhibitions using the "artist + engineer" reference as their modus operandi: pairing up artists with different engineers to fabricate their work.

From the exhibition's press release: "The gallery is a machine for the production of art only in collaboration with others. Users of Production Show are imagined as early adopters of our future Production City ... Production Show will encompass multiple systems, materials and routes of production from industrial to digital, craft to DIY, hammer to iPhone."[8]

The BSoAD has a long heritage, first as an independent school and then within the University. It has forged its own approach to design, embracing the entrepreneurial spirit of its host city. *Architect & Building News* describes the city as both place and spirit that evoke a spontaneous reaction in a write up of the architecture school. It has used pioneering teaching processes – especially since the 1950s with a live project programme to engage students to show how education can play a part in the city. Many of the established architectural firms

78 *Alessandro Columbano*

in Birmingham were founded by graduates of the school during the mid-to-late 20th century. However, it has become increasingly difficult for new design enterprises to emerge, despite Birmingham having the most start-ups in any other UK city outside of London, according to research from the Centre for Entrepreneurs.

Birmingham has a deep-rooted culture of innovation – led by its industrial heritage in manufacturing. As supporters, both BSoAD and EP, played as engineers and artists together in a disruptive process, leading to innovative ideas to set up a production facility for artists and designers. Referring back to Production Show's exhibition, it states "it is by working with our hands on a micro scale that large scale changes occur."[9]

Establishing a space for production

Both EP and BSoAD participate in the growth of the local cultural sector, allowing the organisation to inherit an appreciation of the provisions for the community (or lack thereof). Initial conversations for a production space emerged and developed a proposal called Birmingham Production Space (BPS). Funded with a grants4arts bid from the Arts Council England, the initial proposal was developed with a number of case study visits across the United Kingdom and an online survey to understand the state of the creative scene at that point in 2014. Out of 165 respondents, made up of artists, designers, and cultural organisations, 55% declared they could not access facilities such as physical workshops to develop their work, but 89% stated that it was a requirement for their personal development. This shortfall in access limited the respondents' knowledge and skills to expand their portfolios, to be able to grow their creative business, or to experiment with larger or more complex projects. The impact of the limited access was evident in their annual turnover from their creative enterprises with 73% of respondents claiming turnover below £20,000 and as such being unable to consider their creative work as full-time paid employment. Additionally, the origin of respondents revealed that almost half came from or studied (at HE level) outside of the West Midlands region, having since relocated in Birmingham and the surrounding region.[10] The city draws in a large proportion of new inhabitants from a creative background but the resources and cultural infrastructure required to help them continue developing their practice was limited.

Other datasets indicate a healthy manufacturing and creative sector alongside a future generation; demographics indicate Birmingham as the youngest city in Europe with 37% of the population under 25. The Brum Youth Trend Report, in 2018, reveals insight into what young people think. The most telling statistic in respect to arts, culture, and heritage is that 62.5% believed the arts were important to the city but up to 54% stated that they did not attend or participate in any creative events.[11] There is a disconnect between what they identify as skills needed for the future, to what skills are needed now. The perception is that economic growth in the city is promoted by the local authority but does not provide adequate opportunities for the younger community.

The field condition for a production space

Results depict the barriers facing both the established and emerging creative community, with limited infrastructure available – especially for recent graduates in architecture, the arts, and design subjects. BPS, as an idea, had an ambition to remove those barriers and reform how establishing artistic or design practice is supported by an external facility. Knowledge gathered from the grants4arts research was used to detail a business case for a new centre to house workshop facilities and studio spaces to foster a creative community, facilitate collaborative engagement and mutual learning.

A creative city requires soft and hard infrastructure to establish a sustainable community of creators and consumers that support the local economy instead of exacerbating rapid urban development and the consequences of gentrification. Jan Verwijnen explores the notion of a field condition that aligns itself around common urban problems with architecture as objects that provide a force or influence on its surroundings in the field. Verwijnen states "attention has to be shifted to systems of service."[12]

Universities have undergone a rapid change in their institutional models since the release of statutory limits on student numbers in 2015. Institutions now operate under an increasingly free-market type sector – aiming to attract students in a competitive market with attractive new facilities and buildings.

Rapid architectural developments become catalysts for urban renewal. New zones for living, work, and recreation are formed. BCU has been playing a similar tactic – moving the majority of their campus to Eastside, a former industrial area between the commercial city core and inner-city residential areas. The University is the largest provider of courses in arts, design, and media outside of London, and therefore has a significant student population to accommodate in this respect.

Verwijnen explores the role of universities in relation to their place in a network; "The presence or absence [of a node] in the network becomes a critical source of change in our society."[13] Their ability to impart change holds power to disseminate knowledge and in the case of production, this can turn into the impact of productivity. One of the key problems the BPS research uncovered was the lack of knowledge in graduates to be able to take innovative risks either as an enterprise or as a creative endeavour. Being part of a network allows individuals to experiment and expand. Verwijnen defines this as "innovating without threatening its balance."[14]

Developing the proposal

BPS was intended to be an independent entity born from educational and artistic participants. To achieve its ambition, the team worked with our employer organisations to develop an expanded operation between BCU's Research, Innovation and Enterprise department (RIE) and EP, to receive funding through the Arts Council for the purchasing of hardware and research, with ERDF (European Regional Development Fund) funding and a BCU match to staff a working programme, and refurbish a suitable property to house the facility for three years. To bring a production space into the team's operation, it had to define how the arts could provide the drive to creative innovative solutions by creating a support network for a community to grow and be part of the initiative as it was being defined.

Working within HE led to settling on STEAM thinking – but with a public outlook – to enhance a more accessible social structure in who has access to be creative, and who has a creative impact on the city.

Housing steam thinking

STEAMhouse is a centre for creative innovation. It houses entrepreneurs, sole traders, companies, and citizens to build their businesses, develop new products and services, and collaborate with a melting pot of technology, workspace, and business support. The building contains workshop facilities for members to prototype new products and experiment through material testing. The facility contains digital, wood, metal, and print workshops.

But this project is more than a building or facility, it is conceived as a programme with a broader conceptual strategy for a response to the contextual factors that are affecting creativity and entrepreneurial engagement in the city. Our programmes encourage collaborations

Pedagogy + production space 81

with fellow innovators and encourage members to collaborate with fellow innovators from different disciplinary and personal backgrounds; to receive guidance from industry experts skilled in manufacturing to marketing; receive inductions in new practical skills; attend community and networking events, apply for seed funding, and receive business support to develop product to market; provide new knowledge and workshops for students or staff on emerging STEAM-related topics. While the number of maker spaces and creative incubators has grown in the past decade, these concentrate more on the digital/media sectors or have been started from private organisations and founders. Only 6% were established with government or institutional support.[15]

Building in the city

STEAMhouse is conceived as a space that is open to the public for the public. Architecturally, new campus buildings demonstrate novel approaches to designing teaching spaces but are tightly controlled with electronic access. Even with their location, a campus for academics and students, imply a certain access to these parts of the city. Again, with their own security patrols and branded street furniture or urban landscaping provide physical indications of a pseudo-public space.

The development team made a conscious decision to refurbish an existing building for STEAMhouse away from a campus setting. Digbeth is the former industrial birthplace for Birmingham, but is now its creative quarter (branded as such by the Council) as it hosts numerous creative businesses among light industry and traditional 19th-century warehouses, built around the Typhoo Wharf basin and canal. The simplification of classing Digbeth as a "creative quarter" does not, however, highlight or nurture the entrepreneurial spirit of the city, one backed up by Birmingham having the largest number of patents registered at the UK Patent Office.

Birmingham is a post-industrial city with a large manufacturing sector based on its historical trades of metals and toys (small mechanical or functional trinkets). Its rapid growth during the Second Industrial Revolution attracted several migrant communities to find work in family-run workshops with an interconnected network of suppliers, traders, and crafts makers.

A City of Making report, in 2018, investigated the state of manufacturing in three city case studies. It concluded a rising interest in local production – products and objects or services that are well made for consumers, stating that "the place of production is just as important as the produced object itself."[16] The report also indicated that while universities and technical colleges provide training, there is a lack of flexible space and technology. A more complete infrastructural system would produce innovation-driven manufacturing. Creative clusters need spaces that are conducive to entrepreneurship and support the shift from product development to communication and fabrication.

Manufacturing is an important factor to the city beyond an appreciation of heritage. It builds resilience, stability, prosperity, and well-being. Enhancing manufacturing provisions in the city provide opportunities for sustainable futures, and reduce environmental impact with the agglomeration of industry. Distributed production has the potential for local ownership and involvement. Something that large-scale centralised production rarely does. Urban residents have the ability to construct their city in a way that has not been possible before. All this is connected to Industry 4.0 – an age of mass customisation and super connectivity in our environment.

STEAMhouse as a public work[space]

Industry 4.0 depends on access to this information in order to transform business and methods of production. Universities play a role in opening up this access. But its policy and admission to courses raise social barriers. The intention for STEAMhouse at the outset was to break that perceived barrier – but being visible is not the same as being accessible.

The building is a shop front to the city with its location in a disused car showroom along Digbeth High Street. The existing street elevation has extensive glazing, opening the interior to the city. It has a different emphasis to a campus. The existing building was originally different to an educational building and challenged the conventional architectural characteristics of a University building. Even as a shopfront, its display showcases the interior at a scale that implies production and occupation by large numbers rather than just a few specialist users.

Beyond the "shopfront" lies a series of facilities opened up by dissecting the previous cellular spaces in the rear to create a continuous and visible movement from the street edge to the production spaces. Workflow is improved by aligning a sequence of rooms in line to the production of ideas in a design studio – from concept and investigation, to prototyping, fabricating, and finishing.

As introduced earlier in this chapter, EP uses a series of tactics to represent space and make art public. One of these is by working

Pedagogy + production space 83

"hands on," at a micro-scale for large-scale changes to occur.[17] The design of STEAMhouse considered all of the individual details and how it functions – down to self-made furniture, phasing the completion of the workshop spaces first, before completing the public co-workspace so the team were able to fabricate tables from sheet material and the promotion of a self-sufficient visual aesthetic. Its honest or rudimentary production and material palette is in effect a consequence of the limitation of the procurement process and how funds have been divided as capital equipment – the majority of the expenses required for aesthetic choices were categories in consumables and materials, and hence needed to be of minimal cost to the overall budget.

Public space is incorporated into the layout, balancing the construction budget and the existing typology of a car showroom, the internal plan exploits the larger communal spaces to the front of the building. The diagrammatic plan in Figure 4.2 indicates yellow spaces as co-working and event rooms that face the street and the city beyond while the blue indicates the five production spaces towards the rear. In the centre, our LAB:space presents a democratic approach to sustaining culture by creating civic rooms established for the city to host public talks, meetings, and events. STEAMhouse is creating a culture of production by a communal discussion around making as well as in the making itself.

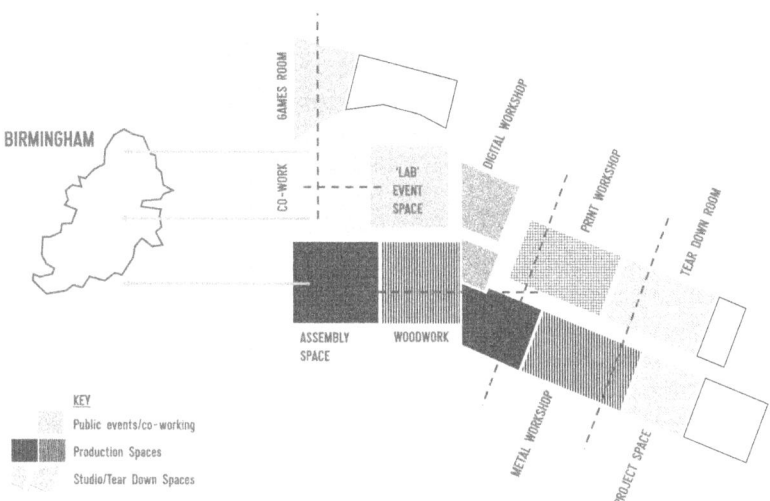

Figure 4.2 Diagrammatic plan of STEAMhouse workspaces.

The LAB:space acts as a producer while its public occupants are the creators. It is actively deinstitutionalising education by the virtue of making it feel like this space is accessible for all. Either in its visibility or in its design, it is to be approachable to enter the front door to ask questions, on how to be a member or participate in any of its events.

Its location is equidistant to the campus, commercial centre, and Digbeth's creative industries. This proximity is important to increase "spillovers" between local connections. Spillovers promote innovative activity indirectly rather than through the direct production of industry by inducing local collaborations. They occur in different formats but the main benefit is that "the mere presence of creative businesses benefit other local firms."[18]

Creative clustering

Connectivity is a key part in achieving the quality and efficiency of a product. A Nesta report on creative clusters uses an in-depth analysis to suggest a three-layered system to provide the right density level of connections to achieve greater productivity and strengthen any sector:

- *Local connections* shared by local firms to help reduce the uncertainties of distant collaboration that may occur with international or new business in a new region.
- *External connections* (outside of a cluster) to draw on sources of innovation located elsewhere, and to embed themselves in global creative value chains.
- *External links* with other local sectors to source novel ideas that can be recombined for innovative new purposes ... disciplines and boundaries become blurred – especially between the digital and creative sectors.[19]

In an educational context, part of a successful thriving student community is to encourage peer networks between specialists so students have the knowledge to create the assignment outputs as well as the soft skills that are essential to an (educational) design process. In STEAMhouse, the connections have been used to connect local artists/ creatives from its neighbouring community, while attracting collaborative projects with larger corporations or companies with a regional physical presence such as Selfridges and Balfour Beatty, or service-based initiatives such as the Deutsche Bank Awards for Creative Enterprise and The Prince's Trust that operate at a national level.

Pedagogy + production space 85

The impact of these connections, and the wider STEAMhouse programme, will be highlighted in the concluding section of this chapter.

STEAMhouse as a public programme

The facility becomes a physical node or hub for members. Applications are assessed by projects under criteria of innovation, creativity, STEAM thinking, and their community engagement. STEAMhouse works as a series of "routes" to define the members' most appropriate need for a project. Routes consist of specially tailored sessions with relevant academics, consultants, and practitioners. Workshops accompany members' individual progress in using the facilities to establish their making abilities.

Workshops are based on design thinking and pedagogic practices used in design or art schools – learning through exemplars, physical testing, iterative design processes, market, or conceptual research. Many members are non-cognate to an art or design discipline so workshops are an effective way to open up an understanding – and in some cases, a first introduction to – how things are made, the supply chain needed and the exercising of design skills. Open-source information is vital for the creative city. Just like open-source data, STEAMhouse opens up educational toolkits and approaches that would normally be on fee-paying courses. They are not designed to substitute or circumvent HE, but recognise accessible, diverse routes into the creative industries.

Institutions are stepping in to play a civic role in society based on the conditions of its context, as a protracted period of political austerity has impacted the public sector to provide opportunities for social mobility and creative enterprise. The programmes at STEAMhouse are not licenced under Creative Commons but still share its ethos. Carlo Ratti describes information as the most valued thing on earth. Information becomes part of the currency that is exchanged.[20] Our STEAM programmes demonstrate the impact education can have beyond "building a new building," as a capitalist model would normally propose as a positive contribution to a city.

STEAM Inc.

Two years since opening STEAMhouse, BCU is the lead partner on an Erasmus+ bid to expand the programme to an international audience. STEAM Inc., as its name, aims to connect, learn, and disseminate the effectiveness of STEAM approach in the HE sector.

The partnership includes six institutions with existing STEAM-based initiatives that challenge the siloed approaches courses can fall into. They are Central St. Martin's College London, Trinity College Dublin, Aalto University Helsinki, Amsterdam University, Dresden Technical University, and Ars Electronica Linz.

STEAM Inc. will produce a new toolkit and publication of case studies from all the partners involved. It intends to promote the value of STEAM and argue for more interdisciplinary working to create stimulating curriculums, and creative competencies that extend throughout the arts and sciences. Its objectives are to demonstrate greater value in the application of artistic skills and a more agile HE sector to increase the arts' contribution to global challenges with innovative approaches.[21]

New Commons for Europe discusses the deinstitutionalisation of education and circumstances around the affordability of design courses. One solution was to modularise education around specific projects to help enact community participation beyond just enrolled students.[22] The STEAMhouse model has the potential to tackle those global challenges but is only possible with a wider support network in place. Despite being over three years old, the project is still setting up the early building blocks to be in a position to tackle global challenges. As institutions are notoriously slow to evolve, there needs to be a sense of permanence to ground all these blocks (partnerships, networks, equipment, knowledge). The building currently acts as the permanent node for its STEAM programme and partnerships that emanate from the community. It might not be modularising an entire curriculum, but there is a concerted effort to take principles of open-source to educate and provide for the city.

Insights from Phase 1

In May 2019, STEAMhouse celebrated its first anniversary. Data indicates impact as follows: 249 registered members, 24 research collaborations, 45 new products or processes created, 85 public events held, and 50 new enterprises supported. Of all the enterprises, 96% are micro-enterprises, 32% from a Black, Asian, and Minority Ethnic (BAME) background and in total an almost equal gender split.

This quantitative impact is valued with meaningful engagement to represent the city and how mechanisms of industry and institutions contribute to the creative culture of Birmingham. User insight from the first phase of funding (2017–2020) revealed how members perceived the programme and facility; "STEAMhouse is BCU, but it is not visually BCU which makes it a lot more accessible, particularly for those that do not think they are the 'type' to engage with a university." The building had created informal working environments for collaboration; "For us as a University it is absolutely crucial to have a place where we can do this engagement, which isn't on a campus."[23] The simplified flow of the building and its operational structure between working and production areas accommodates a mode of engagement that is suitable to share – or open-source – information between members, SMEs, and academics. The lack of hierarchy in the spaces (members are able to access almost all spaces within a 3-minute travel distance) reduces the perception of an overly restricted institutional building protecting its intellectual property – a core currency of universities. STEAMhouse, however, is distinguished by its contrast to conventional campus plans.

Post-industrial cities have a narrative of an unemployed manufacturing base or a dilapidated urban fabric. While significant portions of Birmingham's Eastside and Digbeth areas are under new masterplanning zones, our refurbishment demonstrates a more sustainable approach to encouraging migration and growth into the city without disenfranchising its existing community. Employment in manufacturing is down in Europe but data in the sector reveals a more complex picture where productivity is high and continually improving.[24] A sustainable ecosystem relies on greater proximity to a wider range of resources beyond STEAMhouse. Policy planning needs for smart specialisation to break industry silos and create a distributed model for making that is suitable for smaller individuals and organisations to flourish. Instead of a homogenous, singular industry, the ability to create and prototype numerous products, rather than at volume, relates back to the success of the trinket industry of Birmingham that is cornerstone of the city's heritage today. Fostering a community around making for the 21st century is a catalyst for more inclusive types of innovation, catering for more diverse consumers, ethical production methods, and sustainable impact to avoid a sentimental view of a traditional manufacturing industry.

Much of the initial ambition for STEAMhouse was to house technologies connecting Industry 4.0. Previous revolutions of industry centralised and standardised production, where Industry 4.0 is "set to redistribute it and allow for 'mass customisation' – individually tailoring items at scale …. technologies like 3D printing make small-scale making more affordable and offer opportunities for manufacturing within cities."[25] The report also highlights this manufacturing era with opportunities for cities with limited physical space to counter the pressures of urban regeneration. Distributed production has the potential for local ownership and community involvement and a reduction in environmental impact by reducing travel distances.[26] The building, as a prominent physical landmark, becomes the hub to begin implementing these sustainable goals. This distributed model fits well with STEAMhouse's ambition for members to be innovative in our space through interactive (and not linear) engagements.

STEAM 1.5

Basic architectural principles of interconnectedness have resonated well with our members and users, however, a commissioned summative report from the Phase 1 funding indicates a limited impact in innovative production. STEAMhouse was designated to engage with larger businesses in the low-carbon, health, and advanced manufacturing sectors but this did not occur at the levels anticipated at the start of the project. Their requirements are very different to the SME members that joined. This is evidenced by the West Midlands' position in the innovation index, a metric derived from nine high-tech industries and productivity levels. For its relative scale and population, innovation within the region is proportionally lower than other regions.[27]

With funding of the first phase ending, the University's Research and Innovation received funding to develop its next phase (1.5) for Digital Technologies Enabling Innovation (DTEI) to directly address the lack of impact during Phase 1. The facility remains in the same building but with new spaces refurbished to include emerging digital technologies – virtual/augmented reality, motion capture suites, 3D scanning, material sciences, immersive media/data visualisation software, and advanced CAD/CAM equipment. A new series of educational and creative programmes will support new members' development. This builds on the evaluation of current practices with analogue and physical production and integrates with more demand for digital systems and processes.

The City of Making report highlights the social impact of manufacturing in Europe's post-industrial cities. Learning from its first phase, STEAMhouse 1.5 aims to balance the material culture of an industrial city with the impending environmental and social challenges of the 21st-century city. But what will this look like and how can educational approaches in STEAM facilitate the innovation required to explore those challenges?

Just as rapid prototyping and CAM enabled a wave of open-source systems and the ability for mass customisation in manufacturing, immersive digital media is opening up the possibilities to customise environments/experiences with VR/AR/XR for practical or playful purposes. Carlo Ratti's op-ed on open-source architecture describes it as inhabiting a design "with sentient networked spaces – often through decentralised and devolved systems."[28] Our understanding of the open-source architecture ranges from its application in economic funding to societal engagement, operational standards, algorithmic design, hyper-connected construction, occupancy, and smart data. Since being written almost a decade ago, many of these applications are now part of today's architecture and construction industry – except in occupancy.

Mixed realities (XR) is still a highly specialised technology yet to be used widely. STEAMhouse is now positioning itself as the space for artist, designers, and SMEs to start experimenting with this technology in an environment that encourages risk. Again, STEAM is placing the arts as a key collaborator in how immersive media technologies can be applied to life with engineering and science-based practices. For their user manual #7.2 Policy, EP states to "develop an online presence that is as sophisticated, layered and complex as our gallery space, and offer multiple entry points for different audiences" to create new meaning from digital fragments and articulate new and possible futures.[29]

Artists, designers, and inventors are occupying our digital spaces and social media with their ideas and visions for a more equal and sustainable society. Their ability to allow us to project a future within the confines of our own homes, or to travel to digitised real spaces allow us to experience, and interpret architecture in novel ways that dematerialise our conventional understanding of a very material-orientated culture.

Solutions will emerge with a plural perspective by questioning complex city challenges through interdisciplinary processes between the arts and sciences and investing in immersive digital enabling technologies for phase 1.5 is essential to expand the networks formalised by the STEAM programme.

STEAMhouse as a supporter

There are some important reflections made from the STEAMhouse management and technical team that indicates a clear relationship between building, users, and the creative output. EP's User Manual #7.2 states in policy #16 to "consider design, organisational structures and architecture as programme."[30] Building future networks in STEAM Inc. and future technologies in STEAM 1.5, the spaces in the facility become part of the cultural infrastructure for the post-industrial city as it continues to progress with its urban renewal – driven by "supporters" of industry and artistic identity.

Figure 4.3 Workshop and communal public spaces in STEAMhouse.

In the creative city essay, "New Field Conditions," Jan Verwijnen highlights the cultural and physical bridges needed between two different types of functions you find in the city with spaces of flow (that links nodes and movement), and space of place – areas that provide meaning to people and their everyday life. "With the increased presence of flows in our economy ... as a process rather than [just] as a place that has a history and an identity. Because function and economic power in society are increasingly organised in such a space of flows, the structural domination of its logic essentially alters the meaning and dynamic of a place as we know it."[31]

It is the dynamic of Birmingham as a post-industrial place, and as conduit for prosperous economic flows for the region, where STEAMhouse demonstrates a clear role for a civic University (BCU) in partnership with a collaborating arts organisation (EP) as supporters to play in the development of a creative city (Figure 4.3). The building bridges the spaces (of flows and place) as the facility promotes productivity and making for an active group of the creative community. In doing so, it extends a network and increases exchanges in knowledge to encourage more opportunities for crossing art practice with STEM subjects to be innovative in the global challenges the city needs to meet.

Acknowledgements

The project is indebted to a large team to make STEAMhouse possible. I would like to thank the Institute for Creative Innovation at Birmingham City University for their drive and commitment to funding and developing the project, with a specific mention to Jo Birch and Tom Cahill-Jones and Ruth Claxton at Eastside Projects, Prof. Kevin Singh and Mike Dring for their support at the Birmingham School of Architecture and Design. Further thanks go to Tom Doling and the design team at Associated Architects in delivering the architectural work. Finally, to all the STEAMhouse team staff and technicians that have created a vibrant and creative community for the region.

Notes

1. Chris Rhodes, *Manufacturing: Statistics and Policy*, House of Commons Briefing Paper Number 01942, 12 November 2018, 10.
2. "Is the UK Economy Being Damaged by Our Design Education Policy?" Design Council, accessed February 2019, https://www.designcouncil.org.uk/news-opinion/uk-economy-being-damaged-our-design-education-policy

3. John M. Eger, "STEAM Not Just STEM," Huffpost, accessed September 2018, https://bit.ly/2HCiAuS
4. Ryan Flomerfelt Mather, "Where We're Coming From: RISD STEAM," STEAM With Us catalogue 1 (Fall 2013), accessed August 2019, http://steamwith.us/content/catalogue/STEAMcatalogue1.pdf
5. Stephen Miller, *Designing a Future Economy*, Design Council, February 2018, 52.
6. "DCMS Sectors Economic Estimates 2017 (provisional): Gross Value Added," Department for Digital, Culture, Media & Sport, accessed June 2019, https://assets.publishing.service.gov.uk/government/uploads/system/uploads/attachment_data/file/759707/DCMS_Sectors_Economic_Estimates_2017__provisional__GVA.pdf
7. Andrew Sleigh, Kathleen Stokes, and Hannah Stewart, *Open Dataset of UK Makerspaces: A User's Guide*, Nesta Report, April 2015, 11.
8. "Production Show 2016-2018: Press Release," Eastside Projects, accessed August 2019, https://eastsideprojects.org/wp-content/uploads/2016/05/EASTSIDE_PROJECTS_PRODUCTION_SHOW_PENDING_RESEARCHING_CONCEPTING_PR_2016.pdf
9. Ibid.
10. "Online Survey," Workshop Birmingham: Birmingham Production Space, accessed August 2019, https://workshopbirmingham.org/project/online-survey/
11. *Brum Youth Trend*, Beatfreeks, 2018, 46.
12. Jan Verwijnen, "The Creative City's New Field Condition" in *Creative Cities*, eds. Jan Verwijnen and Panu Lehtovuori (Helsinki: University of Art & Design Helsinki, 1999), 28.
13. Ibid, 18.
14. Ibid.
15. Sleigh, Stokes, and Stewart, *Open Dataset of UK Makerspaces*, 10. London: Nesta. https://www.nesta.org.uk/report/open-dataset-of-uk-makerspaces-a-users-guide/.
16. Ed. Adrian Vickery Hill and Josie Warden, *Cities of Making, Cities Report*, Cities of Making, May 2018, 22.
17. Eastside Projects, *Production Show 2016-2018*, 2.
18. Caroline Chapain, Phil Cooke, Lisa De Propris, Stewart MacNeill, and Juan Mateos-Garcia, *Creative Clusters and Innovation*, Nesta Report, November 2010, Vol 15, 4.
19. Ibid, 40
20. Carlo Ratti, *Open Source Architecture* (London: Thames & Hudson, 2015), 83.
21. EACEA, *STEAM Innovation and Curriculum Report*, Erasmus+ KA.2, March 2019.
22. Flavien Menu, *New Commons for Europe* (Leipzig: Spector Books, 2018), 72.
23. Carney Green, *STEAMhouse Summative Assessment*, March 2020, 21–24.
24. Hill and Warden, *City of Making Report*, 17.
25. Ibid, 21–22.
26. Ibid.

27. "UK Tech Innovation Index," ODI, accessed 26 June 2020, https://odileeds.org/projects/uk-tech-innovation-index/?options=true&datagroup=All%20Technology&location=null
28. "Editorial: Open Source Architecture," MIT Sense Lab, accessed June 2020, http://senseable.mit.edu/osarc/2011_Ratti_et_al_OSArc_DOMUS.pdf
29. "User Manual #7.2 Policy Manual," Eastside Projects – User Manual, accessed 25 June 2020, https://eastsideprojects.org/wp-content/uploads/Eastside-Projects-Policy-Manual-1.pdf
30. Ibid, 6.
31. Verwijnen, *Creative Cities*, 25.

5 Pedagogy + policy
Rochdale reimagined

Sally Stone and Laura Sanderson

Introduction

This chapter discusses an emerging pedagogic approach within architectural education that provides a mechanism to apply the Design Thinking of the School of Architecture to the "Wicked Problems" of local planning. "Wicked Problems" are complex, confusing, and contradictory, and as such are "... distinguished from problems in the natural sciences, which are definable and separable and may have solutions that are findable, the problems of governmental planning – and especially those of social or policy planning – are ill-defined; and they rely upon elusive political judgement for resolution. (Not 'solution.' Societal problems are never solved. At best they are only re-solved – over and over again.)"[1] Through the analysis of a series of projects undertaken by Continuity in Architecture – a postgraduate atelier for research, practice, and teaching at the Manchester School of Architecture, this chapter will examine the particular kind of research-through-design that occurs within the architecture "studio" and how an outward-facing form of Problem-Based Learning[2] can map this thinking onto the planning problems that have arisen through the 2011 UK Localism Act.[3]

Continuity in Architecture deliberately set open-ended "problems" rather than specific projects, and as such have been researching the application of this Problem-Based Learning to local "gaps" within the defined planning policy. The atelier uses this pedagogical approach as a departure from more usual "Live" projects. They have been working directly with the local communities of towns surrounding the city to develop meaningful and productive proposals for the development of the built environment.

The foreground of this chapter is a funded project conducted by the Continuity in Architecture atelier in the Heritage Action Zone

DOI: 10.4324/9781003174080-5

of a post-industrial town to the north of Manchester, Rochdale. The project drew upon 25 years of research-informed teaching already conducted by the atelier, and focused on the problem of the redevelopment of this disadvantaged environment, with special attention to the Historic High Street. This was in collaboration with the Local Council and Rochdale Development Agency. Given that Rochdale is the birthplace of the Co-operative Movement, these collaborative projects seem particularly apposite.

The students' problem-based project proposals and other findings have been presented to the council, they have also been exhibited to the local population in the central library, featured in the local press, and the analysis published as design guides. This has generated new and useful ideas about place that have directly influenced future policies for development within the town. Thus, the collection of student proposals generated new and useful ideas about place, encouraged the community to cherish what is loved and local through an approach that is appropriately cooperative, and importantly directly influenced the future policies for the development of the town, meaning that the insights presented in this chapter are useful to audiences beyond academia.

This chapter is split into four parts. The first section discusses the broader pedagogy of the project and its position as an outward-facing form of Problem-Based Learning. The second section introduces the embedded nature of the collaborative approach within the context of the 2019/2020 atelier projects in Rochdale. The third section explores how collaboration is embedded into the projects with particular emphasis upon Localism and Local Planning. And the final concluding section shows how these "research-through-design" projects have led directly to significant developments in the public planning of local places. It also discusses the ongoing work conducted by Continuity in Architecture, with special emphasis upon how place-based learning can be conducted digitally in a time of pandemic.

Outward-facing Problem-Based Learning

Research-through-design

Research-through-design is an activity signified by the gathering of insights about an object of research; the aim of this process is the collection of knowledge. This knowledge is then analysed and appropriated through the actual design process. Thus, knowledge is gained through the analytical process of design rather than the pure collection of facts. This activity is a mixture of peer-to-peer conversations, interactive discussions, and shared experiences combined with continual reiteration of the process of designing itself; that is, answering the design question and producing an architectural proposal. As part of learning process, the practice of design, a fundamental part of the architectural culture, becomes the first and most significant area of investigation. Its informal structure and the lack of parameters based on the relationship between performance and results means that the creative process is prioritised over the quality of the final product.[4]

The European Association of Architectural Educators (EAAE) Charter on Architectural Research describes research-through-design as a method that transforms particular design solutions into "objects of reflection" and frames them within the wider context in order to generate more than just anecdotal claims based upon a particular project.[5] Since design and research are inextricably linked, there is a direct relationship between knowledge production and the design process. Thus, the aim of a research-through-design project within a school of architecture is to construct knowledge through the acquisition of insight and understanding.

In his seminal publication, "Wicked Problems in Design Thinking," Richard Buchanan explains that "despite efforts to discover the foundations of design thinking in the fine arts, the natural sciences, or most recently, the social sciences, design eludes reduction and remains a surprisingly flexible activity."[6] He defines design (which of course includes the design of architecture and adaptation) as a "new liberal art of technological culture,"[7] and goes on to discuss a type of "thinking that can be shared to some degree by all men and women in their daily lives."[8]

Design and scientific problem solving are vastly different; scientific understanding generally leads to a logical and concrete solution, while more artistically orientated problem solving can generally be compared with the deciphering of a riddle.[9] Within all research, but especially research-through-design, there is a fundamental difference between understanding and examining. Understanding is based upon a comparison while examining requires a penetration of the object, which is more profound. Design is not a linear process; it is a cyclical practice that continually evolves, using informed research to make design decisions that in turn create the need for further investigation; "... like all systematic educational and instructional design processes – cyclical in character: analysis, design, evaluation and revision activities are iterated until an appropriate balance between ideals ('the intended') and realisation has been achieved."[10]

Problem-Based Learning

The "research-through-design" approach has a direct correlation with the pedagogies of Problem-Based Learning. This is a pedagogy that was developed in mid-1980s for the teaching medical students[11] and should not be confused with the notion of "problem solving." Within Problem-Based Learning, it is the "discussion around the problem that is the valuable learning experience, rather than solving the problem itself."[12]

Problem-Based Learning is consistent with the principles of a "constructivist" approach to teaching developed by Vygotsky (1962), Bruner (1966), Bandura (1977), and Lave (1990). Duffy and Savery describe constructivism as "a philosophical view on how we come to understand or know,"[13] they suggest that this creates a set of instructional principles that can guide the practice of teaching and the design within the learning environment. They argue that the constructivist view contains three propositions:

1 Understanding is based upon the interaction with the environment, that is, what is learned cannot be separated from how it is learned and the context within which this happens.
2 The stimulus for learning determines the organisation and nature of what is learned, so the question that is set or the goal of a project stimulates puzzlement within the student.
3 Knowledge evolves through a negotiation of the social environment of the learner combined with an evaluation of that individual's ability to understand.[14]

Applied to the architectural studio, these methods require students to acquire the knowledge that they need at that moment they need it to solve the problem at hand. The practice of combining this with a research-through-design methodology encourages the students as individuals to find out what they need to know within the benevolent environment of the atelier. To a certain extent, the architectural teaching practice of the "design studio" is naturally problem-based, however, research into the application of Problem-Based Learning to architectural education has tended to focus on "non-studio," lecture-based modules like technology and humanities as noted by Banerjee and De Graff,[15] Bridges,[16] and Roberts.[17]

Wicked problems

"Wicked Problems" are loosely defined by briefs and mandates (most commonly those of social interest) that are "ill formulated, where the information is confusing, where there are many clients and decision makers with conflicting values, and where the ramifications in the whole system are thoroughly confusing."[18] Formulated in the 1960s by Horst Rittel as a response to trends that defined the design process as a step-by-step model, "Wicked Problems" are problems that can be resolved but cannot be solved, "at best they are re-solved, over and over again."[19]

It could be argued that all design problems are to a certain extent "Wicked," although the term is most commonly used with those that are complicated by layers of social complexity. Buchanan in his seminar text "Wicked Problems in Design Thinking" concluded that "... design problems are 'indeterminate' and 'Wicked' because design has no special subject matter of its own apart from what a designer conceives it to be ... this sharply contrasts with the disciplines of science, which are concerned with understanding the principles, laws, rules, or structures that are necessarily embodied in existing subject matters."[20] These problems seek an equally complex and often multi-dimensional approach that many professionals do not have the time or resource to effectively deal with in practice, even as part of multi (or even trans) disciplinary teams.

Continuity in Architecture has been concerned with a specific "Wicked Problem" since its inception at Manchester School of Architecture in the 1990s; the challenge of the huge stock of existing buildings and complex "constructed sites"[21] that have outlived the function for which they were built. Their worth is well recognised and the importance of retaining them has been long debated, but if they are to be saved, what is to be done with them?[22]

This idea is discussed by the RIBA Gold Medal-winning architect John Tuomey, who said that "when we say that we think of a building as a permanent thing, that is not to say it must stand intact forever or that it cannot be changed"[23] he then invokes Seamus Heaney, who "has described one function of memory as a kind of disassembly and remaking of the past in which parts of our history are dismembered in order to be remembered in a way which is useful to our present."[24] Creating a place-specific, appropriate, and sustainable future for our towns and cities is a complex problem, which is most pressing in places where residents are keen to maintain the "status quo," a standpoint that architect Elizabeth Timme argues, "makes them vulnerable to developers hawking images of 'contextualism.'"[25]

Rochdale Reimagined

Continuity in Architecture (est. 1993) is a postgraduate atelier for research, practice, and teaching at the Manchester School of Architecture for the design of new buildings and public spaces within the historic city and interventions within existing structures. The atelier aligns itself with the varied contemporary practitioners who discuss the synthesis of situation as the basis for new interventions into existing buildings and "constructed sites."[26] Continuity in Architecture is inspired by a collection of texts that arose in the early Post-Modern period as a response to rigid principles of modernism; these include Thomas Schumacher's "Contextualism, Urban Ideals and Deformations"[27] and Colin Rowe and Fred Koetter's "Collage City."[28] Plus the seminal writing of Jorge Silvetti, who towards the end of the 20th century described the importance of the evidence of the already built: "At the risk of sounding too partisan and biased, I would say that even in historic times documents are not always available, and buildings (monuments, vernacular constructions and public works) are themselves important texts, often providing the first and most lasting impression of a culture. I believe the study of cities can be approached successfully through a minimal model of two interactive physicalities – public infrastructure and monuments – and that the quality of this interaction indicates in great measure the city's level of civic achievement."[29]

In recent years, Continuity in Architecture has worked on the application of these principles in collaboration with local communities, especially those surrounding the city of Manchester. In the teaching studio, the atelier operates with a problem-based approach where students are set an open-ended design problem to create an explicit relationship with environment, circumstances, and history, through the design of architecture. The "programme" of the space is not defined and the students are expected to generate a proposal through their understanding of the needs of the place. This is a departure from the idea of a "Live" project as the students are not expected to simulate practice or find a "solution" but instead to create new contextual findings through their own "Design Thinking." This unique pedagogic approach uses a series of "Wicked Problems" faced by real collaborators with respect to the existing built fabric of their towns.

These problems give a richness to the architectural curriculum, which would not be possible with the more "traditional" brief. The methodology has been developed over a number of years working closely with live collaborators in the form of Local Authorities and Local Community Interest Groups, with each iteration of the approach rigorously tested at peer-reviewed conferences. Over the years, it has become easier to find collaborators willing to be surprised by the answer that a site might generate, and able to understand that there is more value in the "Design Thinking" than in the actual design proposal. In recent years, the "Wicked Problems" explored by the atelier have included: Seasonality in Cartmel, Housing in Bakewell and over the past three years, the Future of the Historic High Street in Rochdale (2018–2019), the Shrewsbury (2019–2020), and Bradford (2020–2021).

In the 2018–2019 academic year, Continuity in Architecture applied their particular approach to the town of Rochdale; a project called "Rochdale Reimagined." The Local Council used their Historic England empowered, Heritage Action Zone grant to fund these problem-based, research-through-design projects. This covered the expenses implicit in travel, exhibition, publication, and knowledge acquisition. The unique application of the problem-based approach was significant in Rochdale and provided insights for both architectural pedagogy and for the town. The learning objectives of the master's course were different from the objectives that might have been set in a traditional client brief – either to an appointed architect or in an educational "Live" project designed to simulate practice. This allowed the students to explore the problem more completely. The "Design Thinking" applied to the problem of the Historic High Street in Rochdale led to a significant exhibition and published catalogue, synthesised and published contextual findings and invitations to do further consultation work in the Borough.

The context of Rochdale, a town on the north-eastern edge of Manchester, is a perfect vehicle for a "Wicked Problem" studio. It is a modern town; that is, it is a place born from the industrial revolution. Rather than evolving naturally over thousands of years, it is a settlement demanded by the needs of manufacturing – and thus, it contains a determined optimism. The town was initially built upon the wool trade, however, cotton arrived at the very end of the 18th century and quickly overtook the wool in importance. Nevertheless, because wool was never fully abandoned, part of Rochdale's industrial strength lay in its ability to switch back to wool when the need arose. Notwithstanding all of this, more than with the great machines of production, Rochdale is known for its egalitarian position, for it is the founding place of the Co-operative Movement. This was grown from harsh necessity, from the need of the local people to feed and clothe themselves in this tough climate.

The town has suffered heavily from post-industrial decline in the second half of the 20th century, combined with a more recent economic downturn, but the council and the people are, as ever, optimistic. The long-culverted river has been uncovered; this provides a crucial moment within the centre of the town upon which other developments can relate to. The new shopping centre is almost complete and the outdoor market has been moved to the banks of the River Roch, thus the town is beginning to be invested with a vibrancy; something that has been missing for so long. However, Drake Street, the historic main shopping route within the town, is still suffering from neglect. It is one of the main gateways into the centre, supports the metro line, and links the river with the railway station. This distinct area has been awarded Heritage Action Zone status by Historic England, who identified a series of sites for targeted regeneration projects to help bring heritage assets back into use to create economic growth. "Historic buildings which have deteriorated through decades of neglect will be restored and put back into use, and unsung places will be recognised and celebrated for their unique character and heritage, helping to instil a sense of local pride."[30]

The future of the UK "High Street" was a question dominating many arenas of British research, even before the COVID-19 pandemic. Two notable reports were published in December 2018 – the "High Street Report,"[31] and the Institute of Place Managements "High Street 2030: Achieving Change,"[32] as well as major funding opportunities including the Ministry of Housing, Communities and Government's 2019 "Future High Streets Fund." Out-of-town shopping centres have contributed towards the decline of the High Street, but this is compounded by the internet. Shopping is now something that can be done out of hours, at home, often while doing something else. So town centres have to rethink how they are to attract customers, how to encourage visitors to spend money and therefore support the local economy, after all, the shopping areas will not be sustained on interactions that are completely personal; that is, "Coffee Shops and Hairdressers." This leads to the realisation that "Encounter and Exchange" will make a massive contribution to the future of the High Street. Visitors need something more than just shopping to attract them into any town centre. There is a need for other activities, for something more to entertain the shoppers. In Rochdale, the Heritage Action Zone status and associated funding will allow the council to develop proposals for truly forward-thinking ways for the development of the town and it is upon this that the collaboration with Continuity in Architecture was founded.

The atelier approach is based upon the synthesis of situation. A strategy that establishes an explicit relationship with environment, circumstances, and history, not just with the building site and its immediate surroundings, but also with the climate, topography, geology, culture, the society that initially used the place and also those that will, in the future, occupy it. The reading of the situation can uncover a layered and stratified narrative, and the understanding of these inherent qualities and conditions can provide clues to the design of new structures. It is through a thorough knowledge and understanding of the existing condition that the architect or designer can uncover the meaning within a place, and this knowledge can be used to activate, liberate, and instigate a new future for any given situation. (Figure 5.1)

Based upon an analysis of the found material, the students are asked to change the situation in some way. This research-through-design mini project is based upon the attributes, qualities, and character that they uncover; as the students make informed design decisions, they also make discoveries about the place. Typically, a programme may ask the student to concentrate upon a specific site, and design the relationship between the three-dimensional nature of the interior, the building, the streets, and the town. They are not yet to design a functioning building, but instead to discuss the qualities of how something can fit into the existing building or the urban pattern and become part of the built environment. They will attempt to understand the relationship between a specific place, itself and its' surroundings, to investigate in minute detail the distinct qualities of a specific place. This actually reverses the more normal form follows function argument, it turns it upon its head, for now, the form of the new elements is dependent upon the form of the existing, so it is not form follows function, but form follows form. This process reveals the true character of the place, it shows how the found qualities have stimulated something new, something that in a way for the moment, completes the place. The RIBA Gold Medal-winning architect Shelia O'Donnell refers to this process as: "Applying a twenty-first century layer of archaeology."[33]

As the design develops, then the true function of the project will reveal itself; the actual programme will be generated through the understanding of the needs of the place. Students are encouraged to continue beyond the development of simple forms, to develop proposals for detail, ornamentation and weathering, and to show how the proposals would age in their context over time. This approach to site is qualified by Bryony Roberts' discussion of "Tabula Plena," the interpretation of which can be stretched to describe a board game or a

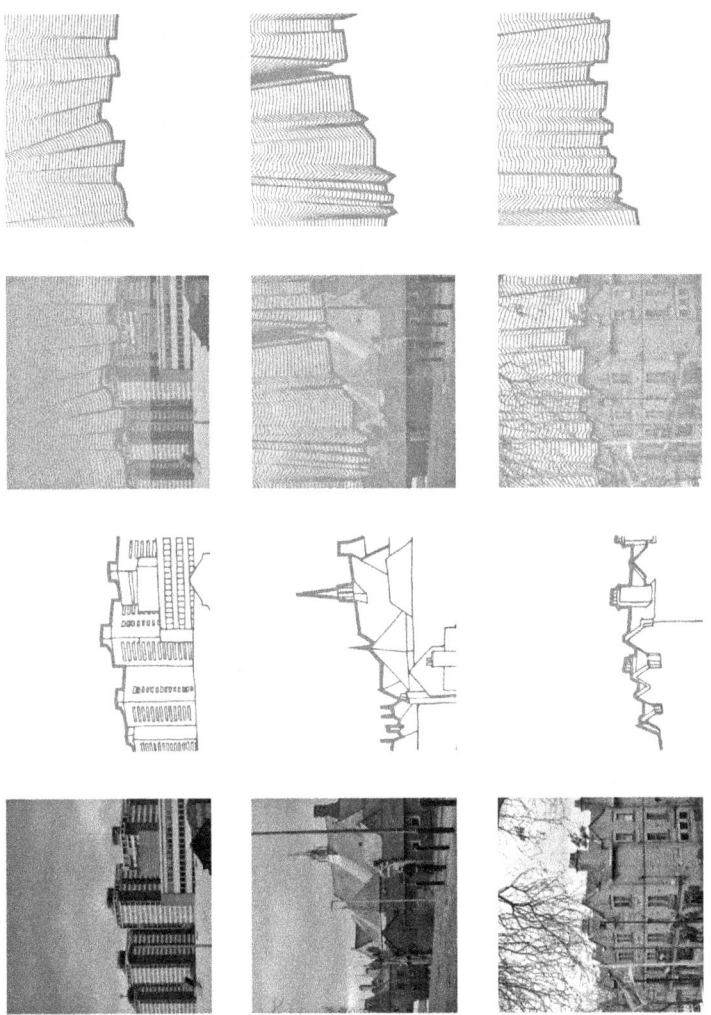

Figure 5.1 Vernacular Analysis of Rochdale, Luke Anderson and Jake Vogtlander, Continuity in Architecture, 2019.

table after a dinner party – "with the complex arrangements of plates, glasses and silverware positioned by a series of social negotiations."[34]

The project in Rochdale can be followed through the design proposals developed by a pair of students who worked very closely together Courtney Ives and Yiting Zhou (Figure 5.2). They began the academic year by examining a vacant site on the edge of the Heritage Action Zone. This small and fast-paced project was a precursor to the thesis project; it was something that immediately immersed the students in the character and nature of the town. The two students explored figure ground as a methodology to create ideal forms, which were then translated into urban artefacts, thus reinstating the site's former use

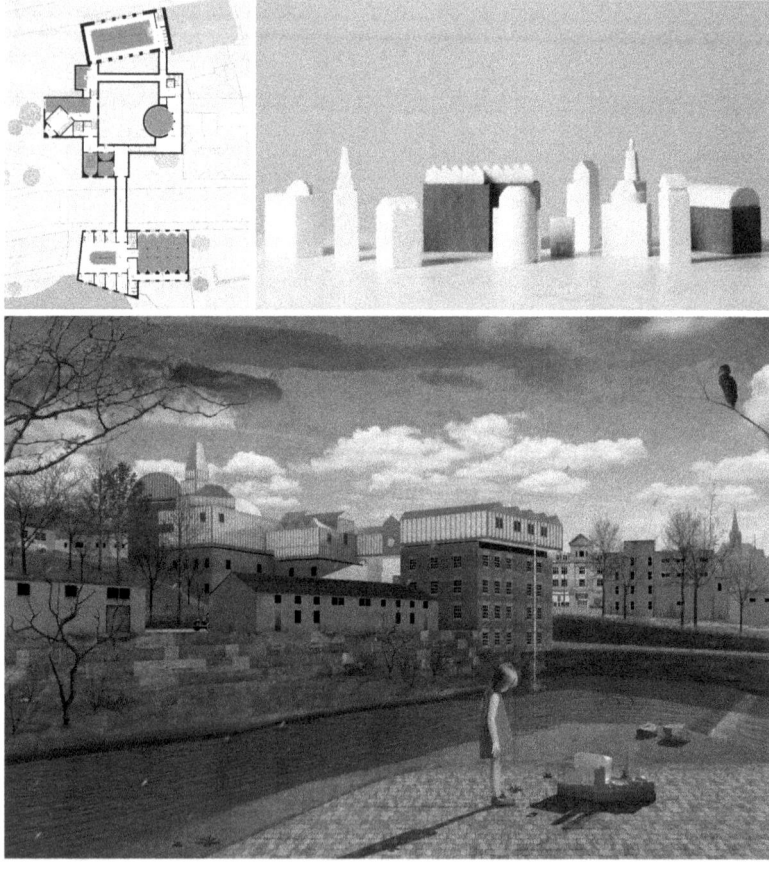

Figure 5.2 Rochdale Bathhouse, Courtney Ives and Yiting Zhou, Continuity in Architecture, 2019.

as a public amenity space. This new-found knowledge then formed the basis of a larger more ambitious project that explored the interrelationship of a series of objects. The students, who were working with a collection of existing buildings and spaces, collaged together a number of local forms to create a new roofscape that echoed the industrial past of the site. They used such precedents as the still life paintings of the artist Morandi, the theories of Roma Interrotta, and the buildings of John Outram, to create a bathhouse on the bank of the River Roch.

Embedded collaboration

Over the last decade, Continuity in Architecture has been developing a particular approach to public engagement. This is a direct reaction to a significant legislative initiative: the Localism Act, which was introduced by the British Coalition Government in 2011 and subsequently became law. Part 6 of this Act of Parliament devolved certain planning decisions to the settlement itself; such that the local residents had the ability to directly shape their own environment. So, for example, potential development sites for new housing could be identified and the capacity for that development fixed. Louise Brooke-Smith, RISC President 2014–2015, stated that "the art of involvement and community liaison is the bedrock of today's planning system and when it works well, it reflects the very best in terms of inclusivity. When managed poorly or not given the respect it deserves, it can result in poor decision making and at worst, some very dodgy development coming forward."[35]

The research cluster embedded within Continuity in Architecture began research in this area through engagement with the Neighbourhood Planning Committees of three small towns in the north of England: Bollington (2016), Bakewell (2017), and Wilmslow (2018). A number of "gaps" in the bottom-up planning system were identified. The first "gap" noted was the "skills gap" in the groups – volunteer organisations lacked design capability and strategic design knowledge to present a clear, illustrated vision for the future of the settlement. Second, and perhaps more fundamentally, there was also a notable "scope gap" in the kind of activities within the remit of the Neighbourhood Planning process, thus a lack of "joined-up thinking." In a recent review of Neighbourhood Planning, Nicholas Boys Smith, the Director of "Create Streets" quoted a senior planning inspector who expressed his frustration at the process: "Half of them are barely worth writing. They just parrot the local authority's plans."[36] Boys Smith goes on to ask: "How can we make for more effective plans?

Some of the answer lies at the local level. The most powerful and effective neighbourhood plans have a very strong sense of place, of what will get built and where. The two most powerful, yet insufficiently used, tools in the Neighbourhood Planning armoury are allocating sites for development and setting out a clear and predictable Design Code for what that development should be and look like."[37]

Continuity in Architecture worked collaboratively with these places to develop new small-town architecture. It was noted that these types of settlements have specific qualities and problems, which are quite different to those of larger conurbations such as cities or large towns. They are places that are desirable, yet strangely overlooked, bypassed, and generally unconsidered; they are too small to be called urban, but too large to be considered as rural. This neglect means that they are often open to architectural abuse. The character and nature of the settlement are sometimes not well considered when redevelopment occurs. Often the charm of the area, something that has attracted people into the place to begin with, is lost with redevelopment; thus, undermining the very existence of the settlement itself. Working closely with the Neighbourhood Planning Committees and through a series of local exhibitions, the atelier worked on designs to grow and improve the places, but importantly, without losing the intrinsic character of the area. These initial projects led the atelier to develop a successful methodology for interacting with public and voluntary bodies.

In Rochdale, rather than a Neighbourhood Planning Committee, the atelier was appointed by the Heritage Action Zone Team (a diverse group who bring their varied project management, arts, culture, conservation, and regeneration experience together in order to influence change in the town centre area), who were keen to understand the position and priorities of the area. The student project was initiated by the Heritage Action Zone Team to explore proposals for a collection of existing buildings around Drake Street, the Historic High Street. Similar to the remit of the Neighbourhood Planning Committee, this task fell outside of the scope of their project and was arguably not specific enough to be able to appoint an architect or urban designer. Students were tasked with the problem of what to do with the existing High Street and looked at a series of existing buildings and complicated sites from the railway station to the town centre.

The architect has certain skills; they understand the built environment, they can read its character, comprehend its grain, and appreciate the inconsistencies. They also have the ability to envisage alternative futures and this ability allows them to suggest different solutions to the ones currently being pursued. Architecture is formed in the imagination and architects have effective techniques for developing and visualising distinctive potentials. Thus, the architecture students were able to develop and depict ideas that maybe other professionals were not in the position to. They can design buildings, propose conversions, and suggest uses that are beyond the project scope and possibly haven't been thought of, and they can communicate these ideas through drawings, models, and sketches, all of which provides the town with liberating ideas, which that can form the basis of much larger discussions. Importantly, these student projects do not replicate nor undermine the work of professional architects, but instead compliment it.

As well as collaborating with local planning teams, the atelier also encourages cross-discipline dialogue. The students worked with academics from different disciplines; including English, Ceramics, and Geography, and relationships were also established with poets, who interpreted the place in a similar manner with vastly differing results (verbal rather than visual). There was an awareness of particular craft-making processes; this practice goes beyond the studio and into the factory, the atelier forged relationship with a terracotta works, a cast-iron foundry, and a joinery workshop. One project by Keqin He used this new knowledge about terracotta to research and interpret the Art Deco details of the Champness Hall, located on the Historic High Street. The project proposed a series of new interventions to improve the circulation of the building and a sequence of spaces for new uses, while also considering construction process and the artistic interpretation of the terracotta details of the existing building. (Figure 5.3)

All of the collaborative projects have been disseminated to the local population, key stakeholders, and relevant professionals. Exhibitions, with catalogues, were installed in the local context for both the Neighbourhood Planning (2014–2018) and the Historic High Street (2018–2021) partnerships. For the project in Rochdale, 50 projects were displayed for two months in the town's Central Library, with prompted questions on postcards used as a way of completing the feedback loop.

The evolution of the research cluster within the Continuity in Architecture atelier has also allowed projects to develop beyond the confines of the academic year and the architectural curriculum. Bollington Town Council commissioned a comprehensive study (with proposals) for the development of its 3 km central road. Continuity in Architecture partnered with local architects, Arca, and other consultant Civic Engineers to produce the report "Reclaiming the Road" (March 2017). This document was then incorporated as a

108 *Sally Stone and Laura Sanderson*

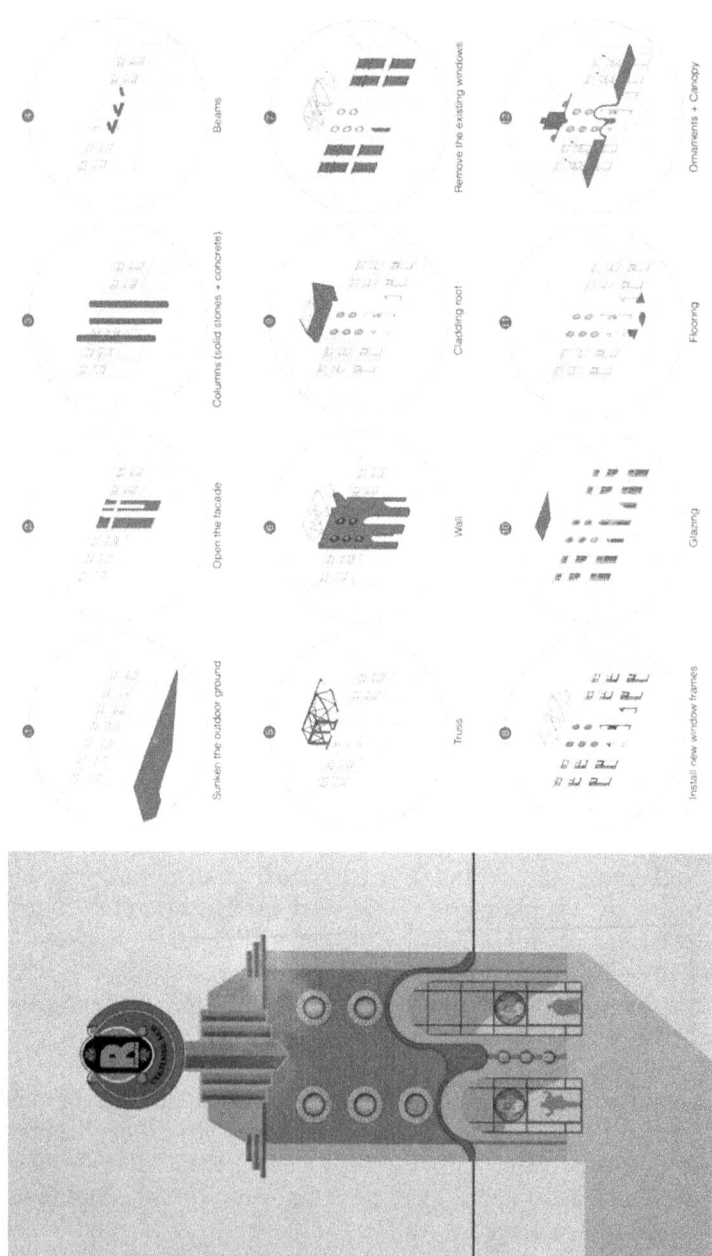

Figure 5.3 Champness Hall, Keqin He, Continuity in Architecture, 2019.

Pedagogy + policy 109

Supplementary Document to the Neighbourhood Plan, also called "Reclaiming the Road," which has been taken forward for consultation and funding proposals. The idea is to reclaim that which has been lost to the transport infrastructure and highways planning and regulatory systems for the good of the local community, the report led to a further project, outside of the curriculum in a small village in Cheshire. The atelier has also collaborated with Roberts Stone Studio to develop small-town proposals for a collection of villages in Cornwall, Oxford, and the Lake District. These proposals are to be implemented, thus the methodology embedded within the atelier has developed beyond the theoretical to the practical advancement of particular places outside of the studio curriculum. Consultancy work with other Neighbourhood Planning Committees has also been undertaken.

Smaller but still significant events have included a series of interventions, including using mirrors to redirect attention to local landmarks (2015), making kites based upon the drawings of local school children who were asked to illustrate what they liked about their town (2016), and the atelier worked with local residents to celebrate local materials in the manufacture of a cast golden stone (2016). In Rochdale, the work completed in the atelier led to further innovative collaborations, including the Heritage Schools Project (2019), which explored the "Design Thinking" of local school children; invitations by the Local Authority to judge the Rochdale Borough Design Awards (2019); and an invitation to collaborate with a national urban planning practice on a project to redevelop land around the Borough's five railway stations (to create 7,000 homes, extensive commercial space, and an £11m cycle corridor (2020)). Each of these satellite projects is another form of place-based participation, engaging a wider audience in the ongoing redevelopment of small towns and villages in the north of England.

Conclusion

Through the examination of a specific project by the Continuity in Architecture atelier, this research has gained significant new insights into an emergent pedagogy for "Wicked Problems." This is contextualised in key literature on "Design Thinking," Problem-Based Learning, and research-through-design. At the beginning of this chapter, the idea that "Wicked Problems" needed to be "re-solved – over and over again"[38] was discussed, this is reinforced by Victor Margolin, who suggests that: "Design is continuously inventing its subject matter, so it is not limited by outworn categories of products. The world expects new things from designers. That is the nature of design."[39]

It was noted that "Wicked Problems" (broadly) and the search for solutions for the "already built" (specifically) were entirely appropriate vehicles for educating architects; theoretically rich enough to meet the academic objectives of the course, yet practical enough to meet the requirements of the profession. Projects in architectural education with a tangible output have been catalogued as "Live" projects for the last few decades, however, a "Live" project does not necessarily operate with a problem-based pedagogy. By simulating "practice," they seek to find an answer, a product, a building: that is a realisable entity. However, as stated perfectly by Mimi Zeiger, "with the power of 'both/and' – that is, Live Projects embrace the best of design speculation, sociological strategies, and construction techniques – comes the spectre of 'neither/nor' – that these projects are compromised by their lack of trajectory within an avant-gardist pursuit."[40]

Through the alignment of the "Design Thinking" that takes place in the atelier with the problems of real collaborators, it is possible to find solutions that might not otherwise have been imagined. By setting a "problem" where the outcome is not altogether tangible, rather than a "project" where the client has specified requirements, this research has highlighted a new line of thinking. The students benefit from the real implications of their work while not being limited by the need to find the "right answer," which aligns intrinsically with Problem-Based Learning. Projects have moved fluidly between academic research tasks, consultancy activity, teaching programmes, and back again – all the while forging links to the community themselves, who actively give and receive knowledge about how their settlement might evolve in future.

The understanding and then adaptation of the conditions of the site can be condensed into an easily remembered saying: Remember, Reveal, Construct. This motto has been developed by the atelier to aid the student while in education and also throughout their professional career. *Remember* the characteristics of the site, look closely at the attributes, explore the nature of what is there, examine the place, and find out what it is saying. *Reveal* the situation, analyse the findings of the investigation, and discover what it means. Use these to exploit the very qualities of the situation. *Construct* new elements that are appropriate to the situation, that heighten the experience of what is there, that become part of the continual evolution of the place.

This Remember, Reveal, Construct methodology[41] is a natural fit to the problems being experienced by the lack of scope in UK planning tasks. The project has evolved again since the atelier examined Rochdale in the 2018–2019 academic year, most notably by the

COVID-19 pandemic, which has added new complexities to the future demands of local high streets and town centres, and also created new platforms for interaction demanded by the necessity of social distancing.

In the 2019–2020 academic year, the atelier continued to consider the problem of the High Street, but this time in collaboration with Shrewsbury, a much more affluent area to the south of Manchester somewhat confusingly governed by both Shrewsbury Town Council and Shropshire Council. The joint council had already produced the Shrewsbury Big Town Plan, a proposal for how to develop the area, and the "testing" of this was the basis of the Continuity in Architecture projects for the academic year. This of course uncovered many different complexities but also a huge number of similar problems to the much more financially challenged town of Rochdale. This was a vertical project in that it engaged three different student cohorts, combining final year undergraduates, with the two years of the master's programme. This allowed the theoretical studies, visiting speakers, and basic research elements to be truly collaborative, while the individual students were able to pursue their own projects within the confines of the programme.

The COVID-19 pandemic arrived just over halfway through the project and all teaching was immediately moved online. This could have been problematic for such a place-focused project, however, the timing was such that most of the empirical research had already been conducted, the students had visited the town on a number of occasions, had spoken with the councillors, local residents, and professionals, sketched and mapped the town, and had taken innumerable photographs for use during the national lockdown.

Generating a completely online place-focused project for the next academic year was certainly a much greater challenge and in the summer of 2020, the atelier was invited to look at the "Top of Town" area of Bradford, a post-industrial city in the North of England. The direct invitation was from the Bradford Civic Society and Bradford Townscape Heritage Scheme (Bradford Council) and was funded by the Architectural Heritage Fund. The Civic Society and the Council were aware of the work produced by the atelier and felt that they would benefit from the sort of consultation that Continuity in Architecture could offer.

The "Future of the High Street" was, even before the pandemic, a problem that desperately needed addressing, but enforced lockdown combined with online shopping is hastening its demise. These areas will not be sustained on interactions that are completely personal; that is, "Coffee Shops and Hairdressers," however, this sense of personal interaction that cannot be acquired through digital communication could be the basis of it – and so Continuity in Architecture have called this project: *Encounter and Exchange.*

COVID-19 has generated more "Wicked Problems" for investigation, such as: what is going to happen in the city centre? Who will be operating on the high street and how will their working methods be affected? How are city centre housing needs changed by home working? And what buildings will become redundant as a result of the pandemic and how can they be repurposed?

Teaching place-based projects online has necessarily meant using digital interfaces that allow for individual tutorials and group discussion. Students are scattered across the world, and as such, drawings, maps, diagrams, sketches, and precedent studies have to be generated across oceans. But we have got into the rhythm of it. Tutorials and seminars do take longer, but also there are many more opportunities to understand the individual context and climate that each student is from. The processes of remote working have increased the possible interactions between the atelier and a wider group of stakeholders, who have attended online tutorials, tours, and talks, something that demands further research when planning future (even located) projects post-pandemic. Collaborators from Bradford Civic Society and Bradford Townscape Heritage Scheme have given the students virtual tours of area while lecturers have provided virtual international study tours online. And of course, the atelier has received international visitors and critics from the luxury of their own living room, something that would have been prohibitively expensive to be done physically. Students have exploited digital maps and picture stores to generate visuals and without access to the well-stocked university workshop, they are creatively using materials at hand to make models, including a collaborative flat-pack model that has been printed and put together all over the world. It was inevitable that many aspects of education would have evolved to be conducted online, but this may have taken 30 years rather than 30 days. Let us hope that when this is over, we will retain all the parts that have worked well and really enjoy the return to located studio-based interaction.

The work by the Continuity in Architecture atelier has presented a cyclical research-through-design process that presents significant steps forward in finding a future for the "already built" through place-specific collaborations. Reflecting upon the nature of these collaborative interactions, it is pertinent to once again reference the opening quote; "societal problems are never solved, at best they are only re-solved – over and over again."[42]

Acknowledgements

This chapter would have not been possible without the collaborators that we have worked with along the way: Bollington Neighbourhood Planning Committee, Bakewell Neighbourhood Planning Committee, Wilmslow Neighbourhood Planning Committee, Rochdale Development Agency, Rochdale Heritage Action Zone Team, Shrewsbury Town Council, Shropshire Council, Shrewsbury Big Town Plan, Bradford Civic Society, and Bradford Townscape Heritage Scheme. The students we have worked with make our work on these projects an absolute joy and their talent and creative thinking is certainly something worth shouting about. Our atelier staff, John Lee, Dominic Roberts, Tim Groom, Alberto Velazquez, Gary Colleran, Mike Daniels, Adam Gray, Claudio Molina Camacho and Johnathan Djabarouti who have given their time and expertise to guide the students with such care. Finally, Professor Graham Cairns and the team at Architecture Media Politics Society who have provided us with the opportunity to present these findings along the way in their conferences in Liverpool (2016), Derby (2017), New York (2019), and Manchester (2020), providing vital feedback to develop our research further.

Notes

1. Rittel, HWJ. & Webber, MM. *Planning Problems Are Wicked Problems*, in 'Dilemmas in a General Theory of Planning, Policy Sciences 4', 1973, 156.
2. Barrows, HS. *How to Design a Problem-Based Curriculum for the Preclinical Years*. Springer Publishing Co, 1985.
3. https://www.legislation.gov.uk/ukpga/2011/20/contents/enacted [last accessed January 2021].
4. EAAE Charter on Architectural Research at http://www.eaae.be/about/statutes-and-charter/eaae-charter-architectural-research/ 2012 [last accessed January 2021], 2012, 148.
5. Ibid, 19.
6. Buchanan, R. *Wicked Problems in Design Thinking*, in 'Design Issues, Vol. 8, No. 2', 1992, 5.
7. Ibid, 5.
8. Ibid, 8.
9. Schurk, H. *The Role of Theory, or What Kind of Knowledge Does Design Contain?* in 'Theory by Design, Research Made Explicit in the Design Teaching Studio', A publication of the Faculty of Design Sciences, Artesis University College, Antwerp University Association, 2012, 73.
10. Plomp, T. *Educational Design Research: An Introduction*, in 'Netherlands Institute for Curriculum Development', 2013, 17.
11. Barrows, HS. *How to Design a Problem-Based Curriculum for the Preclinical Years*. Springer Publishing Co, 1985.
12. Roberts, A. *Problem-Based Learning in Architecture*, in 'CEBE Briefing Guide Series, Vol. 11', 2007, 1.

13. Duffy, TM. & Savery, JR. *Problem-Based Learning: An Instructional Model and Its Constructivist Framework.* Published in Wilson, B. [ed.]. Constructivist Learning Environments: Case Studies in Instructional Design. Educational Technology Publications, 1996, 31.
14. Ibid.
15. Banerjee, HK. & De Graff, E. *Problem-Based Learning in Architecture: Problems of Integration of Technical Disciplines*, in 'European Journal of Engineering Education, Vol. 21, No. 2', 1996. 185-195.
16. Bridges, A. *A Critical Review of Problem-Based Learning in Architectural Education.* eCAADe 24 – Session 5: Digital Design Education, 2006.
17. Roberts, A. *Problem-Based Learning in Architecture*, in 'CEBE Briefing Guide Series, No. 11', 2007.
18. Buchanan, R. *Wicked Problems in Design Thinking*, in 'Design Issues, Vol. 8, No. 2', 1992, 15.
19. Rittel, HWJ. & Webber, MM. *Planning Problems Are Wicked Problems*, in 'Dilemmas in a General Theory of Planning, Policy Sciences 4', 1973, 156.
20. Buchanan, R. *Wicked Problems in Design Thinking*, in 'Design Issues, Vol. 8, No. 2', 1992, 15.
21. Burns, CJ. *On Site: Architectural Preoccupations.* Published in Kahn, A. [ed.]. Drawing, Building, Text: Essays in Architectural Theory, Princeton Architectural Press, 1991.
22. Stone, S. *UnDoing Buildings: Adaptive Reuse and Cultural Memory.* Routledge, 2019.
23. Tuomey, J. *Architecture, Craft and Culture.* Gandon Editions, 2004, 27.
24. Ibid.
25. Timme, E. *Community.* Published in Roberts, B. [ed.]. Tabula Plena: Forms of Urban Preservation, Lars Müller Publishers, 2016, 47.
26. Burns, CJ. *On Site: Architectural Preoccupations.* Published in Kahn, A. [ed.], Drawing, Building, Text: Essays in Architectural Theory. Princeton Architectural Press, 1991.
27. Schumacher, T. *Contextualism: Urban Ideals and Deformations.* Published in Casabella no. 359–360, pp. 79–86, 1971.
28. Koetter, F & Rowe, C. Collage City. MIT Press, 1978.
29. Silvetti, J. Interactive Realms, 1992.
30. Kurik, KL. *Rochdale Heritage Action Zone Project Statement*, in 'Rochdale Reimagined', Manchester School of Architecture, 2019, 4.
31. https://www.gov.uk/government/publications/the-high-street-report [last accessed January 2021].
32. https://www.gov.uk/government/publications/the-high-street-report [last accessed January 2021].
33. Brooker, G & Stone, S. *Irish Film Centre Case Study*, in 'Re-readings: Interior Architecture and the Design Principles of Remodelling Existing Buildings', 2004, 239.
34. Roberts, B. *Tabula Plena.* Published in Roberts, B. [ed.]. Tabula Plena: Forms of Urban Preservation, Lars Müller Publishers, 2016, 10.
35. Brooke-Smith, L. *Foreword.* Published in Norton, P. [ed.]. Public Consultation and Community Involvement in Planning, Routledge, 2018, 0.

36. Boys Smith, N. *Is Neighbourhood Planning Flourishing or Withering? And How Can Communities Do It Better?* Online at https://www.conservativehome.com/localgovernment/2016/08/nicholas-boys-smith-is-neighbourhood-planning-flourishing-or-withering-and-how-can-communities-do-it-better.html [last accessed July 2020], 2016.
37. Ibid.
38. Rittel, HWJ. & Webber, MM. *Planning Problems Are Wicked Problems*, in 'Dilemmas in a General Theory of Planning, Policy Sciences 4', 1973, 156.
39. Margolin, V. The Politics of the Artificial: Essays on Design and Design Studies. University of Chicago Press, 2002, 88.
40. Zeiger, M. *Preface*. Published in Harriss, H. & Widder, L. [eds.]. Architecture Live Projects: Pedagogy into Practice, Routledge, 2014, xxv.
41. This approach is the subject of an upcoming book *Remember, Reveal, Construct: Reflections upon the Contingency, Usefulness and Emotional Resonance of Architecture, Buildings and Context* by Sally Stone and Laura Sanderson, which brings together key essays (including Schumacher, Rowe & Koetter, Boyer, and Cullen), building case studies (including Munster City Library, Universitia Luigi Bocconi, SESC Pompéia, and the Red House), transcribed conversations (including An Fonteyne, Mark Pimlott, Flores & Prats Arquitectes, and MAP Studio), and academics (including Bie Plevoets (Hasselt), Markus Berger (Rhode Island), and Bryony Roberts (Columbia)), Routledge, 2022.
42. Rittel, HWJ. & Webber, MM. *Planning Problems Are Wicked Problems*, in 'Dilemmas in a General Theory of Planning, Policy Sciences 4', 1973, 156.

6 Pedagogy + resilience

Designing resilience in Asia
International Research Program

Oscar Carracedo García-Villalba

Introduction

Cities worldwide are growing at challenging and unprecedented speeds, and in the last decades, they have witnessed climate disasters and extreme weather events at a greater frequency. This scenario requests the need for new ways of teaching the next generations of urban design professionals to tackle the challenges affecting cities and the built environment, such as the effects of climate change, changes in living and working patterns, ageing populations, new mobility trends, changes in the forms of industrial production and consumption, urban informality, or population growth and migration. These and other critical issues further prove that the teaching and practice of urbanism have acquired a much higher level of complexity since it was first instated in 1956 by Josep Lluis Sert. In other words, these issues are affecting our urban and physical spaces. Therefore, it is necessary to create awareness and expose future professionals in urban design, planning, and architecture to think critically and design cities in unpredictable and uncertain scenarios in light of the environmental vulnerability and the exponential consequences of rapid urbanisation and climate change.

This article builds upon the experience of the Designing Resilience in Asia International Research Program (DRiA). It explains how the involvement of multidisciplinary teams formed by universities, researchers, experts, professionals, public agencies, community groups, and industries worldwide has allowed dealing with the complex task of integrating and bridging the gap between teaching, research, practice, and implementation. Teams engage broad and diverse disciplines ranging from politics, science, social dynamics, planning, or design, to explore creative and innovative ways to teach through design studios, partnerships, networks, and collaborative practices.

DOI: 10.4324/9781003174080-6

Teaching urban design in the era of uncertainties

Josep Lluis Sert coined the definition of urban design in 1956 as part of the foundation of the urban design discipline at the Harvard University Graduate School of Design. According to Sert, "Urban Design is the most creative phase of city planning in which imagination and artistic capacities play the important part. (Urban Design) finds the common basis for the joint work of the Architect, the Landscape Architect, and the City Planner."[1] This definition emphasises the broad and diverse nature of urban design, which usually requires collaboration and multidisciplinary interactions between different disciplines to resolve the various and often competing requirements necessary to contribute to urbanism and to serve and support urban communities.

Nowadays, the teaching and research of urban design, planning, and architecture, also understood as urbanism, cannot be oblivious to rapid urbanisation processes affecting cities. The growing complexity of urban phenomena, the impact of new communication technologies in the relationship between the city and territory, and the internationally increasingly important role of the great metropolis are some of the aspects that require architects to develop the most appropriate methods and intervention tools to act and meet the requirements of contemporary urbanism. Therefore, it is essential to understand the role of urbanism as an integrated practice between disciplines, involving a diversity of scales and knowledge, and an intense dialogue with users. In this scenario, more than just defining cityscapes, today's responsibility of architects, urban designers, and planners is not only related to the urban form, sense of order, place and belonging, spatial experience, and urban image, it also has a powerful mid and long-term responsibility in the diversity, social equity, sustainability, resilience and management of our cities, landscapes, and territories, where good urban design configures a flexible and adaptable support framework to accommodate the complexity deriving from uncertain and unpredictable urban scenarios.

The Designing Resilience in Asia International Research Program

In 2014, the Designing Resilience in Asia International Research Program (DRiA) was initiated as part of the Department of Architecture curriculum of the School of Design and Environment at the National University of Singapore (NUS). The DRiA assumes an active responsibility and implication with the design and thinking of some of the most urgent and critical urban issues of our time, climate change, and rapid urbanisation. The platform has succeeded in bringing together more than 25 universities[2] and 400 researchers from Asia, Pacific, Europe, Latin America, and North America as a pedagogical and teaching laboratory to experiment on merging education, research, professional practice, and industry to discuss urban resilience theories and practices.

Setting the scene: The climate challenge

The DRiA starts by introducing students to the discussion of cities' design and planning under the effects of climate change and the environmental implications of rapid urbanisation. The scenario described to students provides an essential understanding of an urban world with most of the population living in cities and urbanised areas where cities, as producers of the 75% of global CO_2 emissions, are simultaneously contributors to and victims of climate change. To contextualise the students with the dimension of the issue to be tackled, the climate goals, agreements, protocols, and policies proposed by the United Nations Framework Convention on Climate Change (UNFCCC), the Intergovernmental Panel on Climate Change (IPCC), and the United Nations Sustainable Development goals, among others, are explained as a global framework to be achieved. Also, scientific studies on the consequences of climate change in the last decade showing data such as the annual average of people living in cities affected worldwide by climate change; the yearly average of climate disasters that have struck our urban environments; the number of disaster casualties; or the impact on economic losses[3] are used to help students to understand the quantitative dimension of the challenge.

Climate change is explained basically as a change in global climatic patterns, mainly attributed to the increased levels of atmospheric greenhouse gases (GHGs) produced by human activities[4] and specifically by human expansion and urbanisation. This is evidenced by four main human activities that are highly related to urbanisation and trigger climate disasters due to their high production of carbon dioxide, which include: electricity consumption and its production through fossil fuels; transportation; building, due to the energy needed to produce construction products; and deforestation that affects the global CO_2 absorption.

Exposing students to this urgent scenario and unconventional topics – usually and still in many cases not included in the teaching of architecture, urban design, and urban planning in universities – allows them to learn how critical and extremely urgent is to build resilient cities in light of the environmental vulnerability, and the exponential consequences and implications of rapid urbanisation and the work they will be doing as professionals responsible for the design and planning of cities.

A theoretical approach: Regenerative design and development, thinking the unpredictable, designing with uncertainty

How we can cope with climate change and its consequences, proposing resilient and livable urban environments, is the central question suggested by the programme. The challenge we pose to students is to explore anticipatory and preventive holistic design paradigms that engender the physical, cultural, and social resiliencies of cities in front of the effects of climate risks due to climate change and rapid urbanisation.

The programme's main principle is investigating regenerative territories as an overlapping of three applied city scenarios: carbon negative (climate positive, nature positive), hybrid, and transitional cities. Through these scenarios, the programme aims to re-examine the role of architecture, urban design, and planning, understanding good design and plans as integrated, interactive, and inclusive frameworks that include but transcend sustainability. Thus, the DRiA works on transformative innovations and designs for regeneration. This means architecture, urban design, planning, landscape, and communities that can – by design – have a regenerative effect on climate, ecosystems, urban environment, and place.

The programme's conceptual framework is based on the theories developed by Pamela Mang, Ben Haggard, and Bill Reed, from the Regenesis Group, and by biologist Daniel Christian Wahl. In their respective publications "Regenerative Development and Design" and "Designing Regenerative Cultures," the authors advocate for a regenerative design, which transforms humanity's impact on Earth from being predominantly destructive to being regenerative, creating a future for humans and all of life by reversing our harmful effects and start to heal communities, ecosystems, and the Earth.[5] In Mang's and Haggard words, regenerative development "describes an approach that is about enhancing the ability of living beings to co-evolve so that our planet continues to express its potential for diversity, complexity, and creativity," going on to refer to co-evolution as the human communities work in partnership with nature, understanding that "partnering for co-evolution requires a whole-system reorientation that connects human activities with the evolution of natural systems."[6]

Therefore, under this theoretical approach, students are encouraged to address the challenge of proposing regenerative urbanism from a system and a nature-based perspective, an anticipatory design and planning in a constant transformation that embraces uncertainty, adapts to inevitable change and is capable of restoring the ecosystem. Thus, the DRiA proposals critically investigate new forms of urbanism as a relationship between two major triads: on the one hand, ecology, resilience, and sustainability, and on the other hand, culture, space, and urban processes. To do so, "reinstatement" and "regenerative" are the fundamental concepts developed by students, not only as of the understanding of recovery or response to climate disasters, usually related to the definition of resilience but, in our case, as the urgent action needed to reinstate and give back to nature in order to revert the effects of climate change by regenerating and restoring the urban ecosystems. In other words, thinking, designing, and planning cities that, beyond sustaining, contribute positively to reinstate and recover the previous status and qualities of the natural ecosystems and the urban milieu.

In this sense, the programme approach aims to transcend the definitions of sustainability, adaptation, and mitigation, and conduct research on the active recovery and reinstatement of the natural and ecological qualities of the urbanised milieu through carbon-negative/climate-positive solutions. This approach aims to generate innovative and creative design paradigms that engender the physical, cultural, and social resiliencies of communities under the effects of climate change and global warming to reach climate-positive scenarios. And the challenge is to match long-term comprehensive, visionary, speculative, and creative urban design, planning, and architecture proposals dealing with mitigation and regeneration, with short-term innovative and adaptive architecture, infrastructure, and technologies transformations that can be scaled-up and replicated.

Three pedagogical objectives to educate professionals committed with the urban environment

To deal with the consequences of urbanisation and climate change, the DRiA programme establishes three main pedagogical objectives linked to resilience-by-design response: (1) to create awareness of the effects of fast-changing, uncertain, and unpredictable environments; (2) to bridge the gap between teaching, research, practice, and implementation; and (3) to generate a platform for knowledge exchange and network collaboration. The three pedagogical objectives transcend the teaching activity integrating knowledge, research, and practice as part of the pedagogy, adopting a research-by-design methodology, and offering a more robust and comprehensive educational corpus.

Addressing contemporary debates in urbanism. Creating awareness of fast-changing, uncertain, and unpredictable environments

In the last decades, we have witnessed natural disasters and extreme weather events besieging human settlements across various continents at greater frequency due to climate change. From earthquakes and hurricanes to extreme temperatures resulting in droughts and floods, these events have wreaked havoc on urban and rural areas alike; they have devastated communities, cost lives, and brought destruction to properties. Rapid urbanisation processes and their effects on climate change are transforming regions, cities, populations, and landscapes into dense and complex environments where resilience and regeneration would be a must.

The DRiA programme's emphasis is on these processes affecting cities and the growing complexity of urban phenomena. It is crucial that, as teachers of architecture, urban design, and urban planning, we create awareness and raise interest among the students regarding the urgent needs in contemporary urbanism related to the effects of rapid urbanisation, climate change, and global warming. The DRiA creates awareness by exposing students to the consequences of climate change in our urban environment, and non-traditional topics in urbanism such as flooding, droughts, earthquakes, and subsidence, focusing on complexity, adaptability, unpredictability, and cycles of change (Figure 6.1). Understanding and intervening in urban contexts affected by climate change require thinking outside the box and designing alternatives with non-traditional design methods and adaptability practices fundamental to their resilience. The programme approach to urbanism constitutes an instrumental point of view for the discipline to show students how urban resilience is an essential area of study in their professional development as architects. By creating awareness of the consequences of urbanisation and climate change, the DRiA promotes innovative and creative design paradigms that encompass cities' physical, environmental, social, cultural, and economic resilience in unpredictable scenarios.

122 *Oscar Carracedo García-Villalba*

Figure 6.1 Resurgent City. Repair, Regenerate, Revive: Urban design proposal for Chennai (India) addressing water scarcity and water pollution, by Li Jinzhe, Liu Zhilin, Mo Wenyi. DRiA-National University of Singapore.

Bridging the gap between teaching, research, practice, and implementation

For the disciplines of architecture, urban design, and urban planning, whose fundamental and ultimate goal is, in most cases, real implementation of projects and plans, it is essential to integrate professional practice, research, and teaching to "bridge the gap" between academia and the "real world." The DRiA experience in this integration has revealed to be crucial to convey to students the reality and proximity to the concepts and tools that professional practice requires.

For the DRiA programme, addressing real-world problems is critical due to the global urgency of the themes discussed. The fact that the programme's primary concerns and objectives are not in a silo or unique to a discipline alone requires a more complex, cross-disciplinary, and holistic approach. This calls for combining knowledge on different topics related to climate change with real-life case studies that allow students to understand the different approaches to each topic.

In this sense, the DRiA programme understands the teaching of urban design, planning, and architecture not just as the act of lecturing to students, but mainly as the combination of teaching and the application of design-based research and knowledge to professional practice. In this way, the programme introduces students to a professional approach to urbanism, valuing teamwork, and developing autonomy, with an essential individual component of integrated outcomes within a group work. This also helps to shift the student's approach to urbanism from a self-aware, top-down perspective focused on formal and functional outcomes to formulate strategic frameworks that integrate theories, concepts, models, tools, empirical material, and the research findings needed in the city project.

Amplifying urban design: Generating a platform for knowledge exchange and network collaboration

The interdisciplinary structure of the DRiA offers a unique platform that gathers knowledgeable international experts on resilience to lend their expertise and encourage the exchange of innovative and practical ideas for future resilience. Also, professors and students from all over the world contribute to the debate on how to create strategies to adapt to and mitigate the effects of climate change through diverse approaches such as design, planning, technology, management, policies, or community involvement.

This platform aims to amplify the urban design discourse, intended to suggest different ways for the students to understand and connect with the current urbanisation questions at the global, regional, and local levels. This allows the students to learn from different sociocultural environments, ideas, visions, and backgrounds, linking theories to real practices and broadening their understanding of urban design beyond standard discourses.

The DRiA serves as a medium of exchange of knowledge and expertise for students, where they are exposed to different approaches and the less equipped universities get to learn from the better trained through their expression of ideas, while the more equipped learn from the less equipped on how to approach the topics more pragmatically. In other words, the exchange of ideas helps the students to study the same issues through different perspectives.

Four methods to design in the era of uncertainties

To develop the pedagogical objectives under the regenerative approach, the programme works on four complementary methods.

Learning from experience, learning by doing

The DRiA emphasises the ideas of "learning from experience" and "learning by doing." There is a need to expose students to the personal experience of urban spaces and the city's recognition as a first-hand learning process towards a self-generated urban culture. Learning from experience is achieved through the personal experience in field trips, incorporated in the agenda of the DRiA as the basis to build a solid foundation on urban culture. Learning from experience provides students with an understanding of the urban realities and the methodological tools to approach the necessary historical, contextual, and cultural backgrounds as the basis for the study and reflection upon any urban design, planning, or architecture project.

The field trips and overseas programmes promote students' critical thinking and amplify their understanding of contextual specificity in architecture and urban design. The experience of the DRiA in cities in China, Philippines, Indonesia, Thailand, and India has helped expose students to unconventional discourses on urban topics such as resilience, water scarcity, and management, among others. Such trips present the students with an opportunity to interact with local people, as they prove to be of great benefit and help to incorporate local cultural components and ideas into the design process. Community members are involved in the grassroots processes, becoming co-learners with students and faculty to create a coextensive learning community, broadening the learning environment, and multiplying its value.

Learning by doing is achieved using the design project as a learning tool and a source of knowledge. This approach suggests comparative thinking (reflection), interpretive analysis (reading), and the intentional proposal (interpretation) as parts of the "act of doing" and as inseparable parts of the design process. Learning by doing allows students to have a professional thinking approach as a form of learning, exploring the relationship between the project and its implementation, or "how to make designs possible."

Active learning, co-learning, and design-based learning

Active learning and lively, engaged, and interactive sharing sessions through active debates and dynamic feedback are crucial parts of the

DRiA methodology. This approach is combined with cooperative learning, where students work in teams on projects under conditions that generate both positive mutual interdependence and individual accountability. The DRiA programme encourages student-centred learning where the students are engaged in learning activities that not only benefit themselves but also encourage peer-to-peer learning.[7]

The primary aim of the DRiA initiative is to provide anticipatory solutions through design. In urban planning, Shepherd and Cosgrif refer to design-based learning as a "bridge between planning education and planning practice."[8] In the DRiA, design plays a vital role that goes beyond buildings, landscapes, and places, and includes the thinking of organisations, processes, and programmes. Hence, design practices are combined with other fields, including science, engineering, education, health, social services, and public policy, among others. Cooperation with other disciplines is essential for the DRiA initiative to bring the multidisciplinary vision required in the contemporary urban design and planning processes.

Research by design

The DRiA method encourages "Research by Design." As defined by Jorgen Hauberg and the research committee at the European Association for Architectural Education,[9] "Research by Design" is understood as the various ways design and research are generally interconnected when new knowledge about the world is produced through the act of designing. Therefore, research by design is any kind of inquiry in which design is a substantial part of the research process. In research by design, the architectural/urban design process forms a pathway through which new insights, knowledge, practices, and products come into being.

The DRiA "Research by Design" approach generates critical inquiries through design work, which may include realised projects, proposals, possible realities, and alternatives, as well as verbal and non-verbal outputs and discourses that are proper for the urbanism discipline practice and are discussable, accessible, and useful to peers and others.

Learning through design games

This methodology explores the potential of design games as a pedagogical teaching approach, reflecting on their value in an interdisciplinary and educational context. Using the city as a space of play, the specific interest helps students explore processes and forms of urbanisation and their relationship to urban resilience, designing for contingency, unpredictability, and change.

The use of games in education has a long history, especially in the participatory design approach. Habraken, Sanoff, and Hamdi[10] have developed the design games approach as a means for negotiation and sharing, emphasising the processes rather than the solutions. As Sanoff points out, these games can be used in the design studio context with the educational objective of facilitating decision-making, self-management, and understanding of complex contexts.[11]

The DRiA design game method helps students see how the diverse components of city systems are interconnected and which decisions are essential to adapting urban space to unpredictable changes in climate patterns while providing a platform for the students to engage, collaborate, foster interaction, and improve their decision-making.

DRiA: Designing regenerative and decarbonised futures, working with unpredictabilities towards nature-positive cities

The focus of the DRiA programme is on design and the city as drivers of resilient change, which requires the resetting of methods and intervention tools, and the development of new paradigms to rethink the role of design in order to meet the challenges of global development and contemporary urbanism. Working in real specific cities, sites, and scenarios, the programme discusses the design of the city-region, understanding that the environmental consequences and implications of rapid urbanisation and climate change transcend administrative boundaries.

Statement and hypothesis: Buildings as synthetic trees, cities as synthetic forests

As mentioned before, the proposals developed in the frame of the DRiA adopt the regenerative theories through different approaches in designing carbon negative (climate positive – nature positive) and regenerative systems of different scales, from building systems to urban design and city planning.

The following project, developed under the framework and premises of the DRiA, explores the notion of urban design and architecture as alternative mediums to absorb carbon dioxide (CO_2) from the atmosphere, becoming carbon sinks that help mitigate the impacts of climate change. The project also exemplifies some of the methods used in the programme, focusing particularly on design-based learning, learning from experience, learning by doing, and research by design (Figure 6.2).

The project statement is a reaction to a Singaporean bank advertisement published on *The Straits Times* newspaper stating that cities and buildings will never produce oxygen and store carbon, unlike forests. CO_2, the most abundant GHGs that cause global warming and climate change, has been rising rapidly due to the increase of anthropogenic activities. Several studies demonstrate that trees alone are no longer sufficient to absorb and reduce carbon in the atmosphere to meet the UNFCCC goals and address climate change.[12] Hence, there is an urgent need to find alternative approaches to remove CO_2 from the atmosphere to mitigate climate change and prevent climate disasters. The project statement suggests that ending climate change starts with architecture and the city.

The project revolves around two research questions: whether cities and architecture can contribute to absorb and remove CO_2 from the atmosphere permanently and be transformed into carbon sinks; and whether cities convert the captured CO_2 into natural and economic resources.

To answer these questions, the project hypothesises that buildings and cities can become "synthetic trees and forests" by integrating different strategies and systems to store and absorb CO_2 from the atmosphere. Following this idea, the proposed design objective is to use cities as mediums to combat climate change, where architecture contributes to nature and takes the role of creating a new carbon-negative landscape. By working with nature-based solutions, the carbon threat can be converted into an opportunity, and excess of CO_2 in the atmosphere can be transformed into resources and assets to creating productive carbon-negative cities and mitigating the effects of climate change.

"Form follows function," coined by Louis H. Sullivan, was one of the key thoughts and strategies that shaped today's modern cities. Later, concerning the environment, Charles Correa created the statement "Form follows climate," advocating that buildings should respond to the climate and approach the different systems passively, reducing the need for additional energy. The project suggests a powerful and innovative statement that revises the architectural principles. The notion of "Form follows carbon" where cities and buildings are designed to actively remove carbon dioxide from the atmosphere, creating carbon-negative cities and a new decarbonising urban culture. In this way, a carbon culture will offer a compelling long-term way

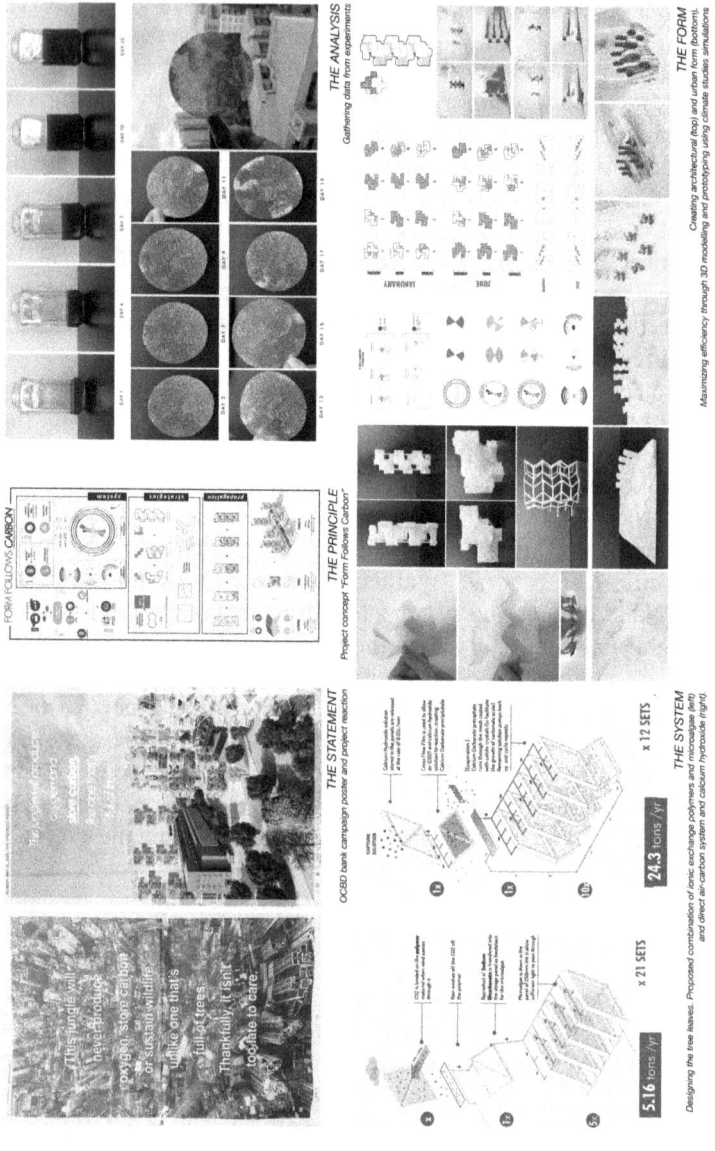

Figure 6.2 Development of the DRiA methodology: statement, principle, analysis, system, and form by Chey Yi Ting. DRiA-National University of Singapore.

Pedagogy + resilience 129

to mitigate climate change and eventually return to the pre-industrial levels of carbon dioxide and a more sustainable and livable planet.

Discourse and analysis: The synthetic forest strategies

According to the World Green Building Council,[13] 39% of the global energy-related CO_2 emissions come from buildings and the construction process. The synthetic forest proposal capitalises on carbon by integrating CO_2 absorbing strategies as building systems to create carbon sink cities. Three different techniques and approaches are analysed.

Biological approach, green and blue CO_2 sequestration

There has been increasing recognition and evidence that microalgae are the most effective biological species for capturing carbon through photosynthesis (Sayre, 2010). Compared to other plants that require many years to grow, microalgae require less time and physical space to grow, increasing the photosynthesis rate. Conclusions from studies show that algae can remove 400 times more CO_2 than a regular tree.[14]

To understand this approach, aligned with the learning by doing methodology, the student developed a microalgae growth experiment to measure and get data from the growing process, time, maintenance, and its resilience.

Chemical approach, build as you capture

One of the most effective ways of sequestrating CO_2 is to store it permanently in a solid status instead of gaseous, where CO_2 is released back again into the atmosphere. Carbonation is a method where CO_2 chemically reacts to form calcium carbonate. Calcium carbonate is the biggest repository of carbon on the planet. It can be easily found in many forms in nature, like limestone, marble, or even in the ocean like seashells and corals.[15]

The project suggests that mimicking nature may be an efficient approach to sequestrate carbon dioxide from the atmosphere. The study investigates ways of accelerating the carbonation process, usually a prolonged natural process. Through an experiment on the rate and formation of carbonate scales, having a constant flow of saturated water with calcium carbonate at approximately 40 degrees Celsius, calcite, the hardest form of calcium carbonate, is formed in pipes.[16] With these factors, it is possible to absorb 1 kg of CO_2 in the form of calcium carbonate by allowing the solution to flow continuously for 53 days.

For this approach, the student also developed a calcium carbonate growth experiment to observe the final effect and product and quantify the amount of CO_2 absorbed. In this case, a solution of calcium hydroxide (CaOH) precipitates into calcium carbonate ($CaCO_3$) when CO_2 is introduced. The evaporation of the solution forms the calcium carbonate scale, which contains and stores the CO_2 and grows as carbon is captured.

Direct air carbon systems

Finally, the proposal also studies a third approach based on carbon engineer technologies for capturing CO_2 directly from the atmosphere that has proved to be more efficient than the photosynthesis process by trees in the carbon absorption. The proposal suggests that future architectural systems could incorporate artificial photosynthesis strategies applied at different scales, enabling the absorption and storage of carbon. These carbon engineer technologies vary, and while some systems use positive ionisation technologies to draw pollutants such as black carbon from the atmosphere, others integrate ionic exchange polymers filters. Coated with sodium carbonate solutions, the filters react to and absorb CO_2, forming sodium bicarbonate, a harmless chemical product found in baking soda that can be used to feed algae.

Parameters: Design as a result of quantitative research and experimentation

The fundamental approach of the design process is to explore efficient methods and forms that facilitate the carbon capture process. Thus, the project explores the design of cities and architecture as an alternative tool to capture CO_2 in three scales: the systems, the form, and the city.

As previously mentioned, the design revolves around the idea of form follows carbon, which aims to explore different systems to maximise the carbon capture. Three different approaches are explored to develop the idea and the concept of the synthetic forest.

Synthetic leaves: The systems

As seen in the analysis, CO_2 can be absorbed using different methods and technologies. The proposal suggests combining and integrating techniques in two different systems to accelerate the processes and efficiency.

The first system involves a continuous process of CO_2 absorption as feedstock for photosynthesis combining the biological approach and the ionic exchange polymers. This system is a close loop process where the CO_2 captured by the polymer-ionic exchange in the form of sodium bicarbonate is used to grow the microalgae. Microalgae will absorb and transform the CO_2, as studies have shown that using soluble carbonates as a carbon source for growing algae is more effective than using direct CO_2 gas from the atmosphere.[17] In addition, microalgae treat the water so that it can be recycled and pumped back to the polymer system to restart the process.

According to the data from analysis and experiments, the student concluded that 21 sets of the design prototype of this combined system could capture 5.16 tons of CO_2 per year.

The second system involves permanent storage of CO_2 by using it as a building material combining the chemical approach and the direct air-carbon system in the form of a cross-flow film filter. The filter allows putting in contact the calcium hydroxide solution and the air to absorb the CO_2 in the form of calcium carbonate.

In this case, according to the analysis, the experiment, and the data derived, one prototype set can capture approximately 24.3 tons of CO_2 per year.

Synthetic trees: The buildings

The second approach involves the student exploring of a mixed-use prototype typology to maximise the surface area in contact with the atmosphere. Architectural spaces are designed to capture carbon most efficiently while flexible to adapt to different programmes.

The origami folding technique is used to propose a building skin that increases the surface area in contact with the atmosphere, creating planes that face different directions to respond to different climatic conditions.

The resulting form of the building envelope comes from, on the one hand, the analysis and understanding of the climatic conditions of the site and the requirements for each of the previous systems. And on the other hand, from an in-depth exploration of the module form, its placement, and stacking to maximise sunlight and wind exposure. An exhaustive 3D prototype modelling resulted in a spiral staggering as the most efficient form of passive architecture to allow cross-ventilation and increase the wind-tunnel effect to maximise the carbon capture.

According to the data obtained from the experiments with the prototype systems, one synthetic tree will absorb the same amount of CO_2 as approximately 50,000 mature trees.

Synthetic forest: The city

Finally, the synthetic forest city will take the new carbon-capturing architectural prototype as the basis for creating flexible, hybrid, complex, and integrated carbon-negative urban environments. The proposal rethinks how the city should be designed, adapting to climate change and playing an active role in mitigating its effects. The biomimicry and nature-based solution proposed is a new flexible and adaptable building envelope that adapts to new typologies and diverse uses and existing buildings, transforming them into carbon-negative and nature-positive structures.

With the objective to absorb the maximum amount of CO_2 from the atmosphere, the exposure and contact with air and sun, and the "collaborative" interaction between buildings, constitute the main drivers of the urban design layout. Using 3D urban prototyping, wind, and sunlight simulation software, the project did an in-depth study of the most efficient building layout to increase their performance, maximising the site's climatic advantages and characteristics. Thus, for this proposal, buildings are the new city interfaces and the structures of the new carbon sink city (Figure 6.3).

As a result of the urban layout of the "synthetic trees" and their interaction, and following the experiments' carbon absorption data, the proposal can absorb about 14,800 tons of CO_2 per year, the equivalent to one million trees approximately. Thus, if the urban prototype is scaled-up throughout Singapore and approximately 160,000 synthetic trees are implemented, forming an island-wide synthetic forest, the country's yearly CO_2 will be absorbed.

Responding to real-world cases, linking to government and public agencies

The DRiA focus revolves around comprehensive proposals that endorse strategies combining solutions for specific sites and city-wide urban challenges, liaising with local governments and public agencies to tackle their needs.

In this case, this proposal uses Singapore as a test bed for the proposed prototype. Although known as the "city in a garden," Singapore cannot be claimed as "green" or sustainable because of its role as one

Pedagogy + resilience 133

Figure 6.3 The Synthetic Tree & The Synthetic Forest: carbon-negative and nature-positive architecture and cities, by Chey Yi Ting. DRiA-National University of Singapore.

of the largest trading hubs in Asia, and due to the lack of natural resources and high dependency on imports from all over the globe. According to the 2018 Singapore National Environment Agency data, it can be observed that Singapore is one of the largest emitters of CO_2, at a ratio of 10.31 tons per capita in 2014 without including the aviation and marine emissions for international bunkers. Counting the emissions of these two sectors, in 2014, Singapore emitted 194 million tons of CO_2, equivalent to 35.1 tons of CO_2 per capita, with only 0.24 million tons of carbon sink capacity. Thus, Singapore urgently requires the implementation of mitigation strategies to avoid further impacts. It is crucial that the country takes the initiative to restore and regenerate the city through decarbonising approaches.

The project takes the former Pasir Panjang power station site to explore the development of a nature-positive and decarbonised city. The state property district was suggested by the Urban Redevelopment Authority (URA) and the Singapore Land Authority (SLA) to be re-imagined for the next 15–20 years as part of a new urban model for the Greater Southern Waterfront. In this sense, the project transforms the site, which used to be a carbon emissions source, into a CO_2 absorptive city. A prototype model that can be scaled-up and replicated along the waterfront and other parts of the city to achieve a nature-positive and decarbonised future for Singapore.

Concluding remarks

There is a need to train highly qualified and excellent architects, urban designers, and planning professionals who will be indispensable for implementing outstanding physical designs and city-scale urban projects adapted to a dynamic, uncertain, and highly complex urban environment, promoting local identity, environmental values, and a commitment to social equity.

The teaching of urbanism, that should be done by specialised professors with professional practice background and experience, has to be reformulated to create environmental awareness by introducing the urgent needs posed by the contemporary consequences of urbanisation and climate change as the main object of study. This orientation towards real and urgent projects, developed through research by design methods, initiates students to a professional approach to urban and architecture design while generating a higher level of commitment towards the environmental and social impact of the architect's profession. This also reveals to students the urgent need for integrated multidisciplinary and grounded teamwork, shifting from formal and functional individualistic perspectives to the design of frameworks, processes, and strategies.

As part of the Designing Resilience in Asia International Research Program, students are designing projects and plans that explore responses to critical urban issues of our time such as mobility and CO_2 emissions, food security, water scarcity, sea-level rise, flooding, or waste management. They translate the response to the impacts of climate change and urbanisation into nature/climate-positive design opportunities that contribute to the advancement of urbanism as a discipline.

The challenge of discovering how urbanism can adapt to and mitigate the effects of climate change, but also reinstate, recover, and return the natural and ecological qualities to the urban milieu through

Pedagogy + resilience 135

the design of anticipatory resilience measures and strategies, has been translated into design and planning proposals for sites all over southeast Asia. By thinking creatively and holistically, these projects (and other ongoing projects) are coming up with nature-based, innovative solutions, tools, and methods, while discussing the role of urban designers, architects, and planners as responders to a call for building anticipatory resilience measures and strategies through designs.

Learning urbanism is a long-life project. In this long journey, our responsibility as educators with the coming generations is, on the one hand, to create a positive learning environment in their early stages as students, and on the other hand, to leave a positive impact and an intellectually honest imprint that engages their future professional work in contributing to the reinstatement of our cities' natural values.

Acknowledgements

I would like to thank Gabrielle Liew and Chey Yi Ting, students of the National University of Singapore, for the commitment and passion devoted and the tireless and impressive work done. My special appreciation and gratitude to Chey Yi Ting, author of "The Synthetic Tree" proposal, used in this article to explain and illustrate the DRiA methodology, approach, and principles.

Notes

1. Alex Krieger and William S. Saunders, eds. *Urban design* (University of Minnesota Press, Minneapolis, 2009).
2. http://designingresilience.com/. The DRiA network is an interdisciplinary collaboration between universities across the world, including: Anna University (India), Bangladesh University of Engineering and Technology (Bangladesh), BRAC University (Bangladesh), Centre for Environmental Planning and Technology (India), City University of New York (USA), Curtin University (Australia), De La Salle College of Saint Benilde (Philippines), Institut Teknologi Bandung (Indonesia), International University of Catalonia (Spain), King Mongkut's University of Technology Thonburi (Thailand), Kyushu University (Japan), Louisiana State University (USA), National Cheng Kung University (Taiwan), National University of Singapore (Singapore), PVP College of Architecture (India), RMIT (Australia), Rotterdam University of Applied Sciences (The Netherlands), South China University of Technology (China), Technological and Higher Education Institute of Hong Kong (Hong Kong), TU Darmstädt (Germany), Université de Montréal (Canada), University of Pennsylvania (USA), University of Hawaii (USA), Universite de Montreal (Canada), University of Pennsylvania (USA), and Universitas Katolik Soegijapranata (Indonesia).

3. Yearly average data from CRED. Natural Disasters 2018. Brussels: CRED; 2019 EM-DAT file.
4. Lexico Dictionary, "Definition of Climate Change by Lexico", accessed 8 November 2019, https://www.lexico.com/en/definition/climate_change
5. Daniel Christian Wahl, "Designing Regenerative Cultures", *Permaculture Magazine*, 2016, https://www.permaculture.co.uk/articles/designing-regenerative-cultures.
6. Ben Haggard and Pamela Mang. *Regenerative development and design: a framework for evolving sustainability* (John Wiley & Sons, Inc., Hoboken, New Jersey, 2016).
7. Michael Neuman, "Teaching Collaborative and Interdisciplinary Service-Based Urban Design and Planning Studios." *Journal of Urban Design,* 21, No. 5 (2016): 596–615.
8. Anne Shepherd and Bryna Cosgrif, "Problem-Based Learning: A Bridge between Planning Education and Planning Practice." *Journal of Planning Education and Research,* 17, No. 4 (1998): 348–357.
9. Jørgen Hauberg, "Research by Design – A Research Strategy." *Lusofona Journal of Architecture and Education*, [S.l.], No. 5 (March 2012): 46–56. ISSN 1646-6756.
10. N. John Habraken and Mark D. Gross, *Concept design games* (Cambridge, MA: MIT Press, 1987); Henry Sanoff, *Design games* (Los Altos, CA: Kaufmann, 1979); Nabeel Hamdi, *Small change* (London: Earthscan, 2004).
11. Ceridwen Owen, Kim Dovey, and Wiryono Raharjo, "Teaching Informal Urbanism: Simulating Informal Settlement Practices." *Design Studio, Journal of Architectural Education*, 67, No. 2 (2003): 214–223.
12. Lena R. Boysen, Wolfgang Lucht, Dieter Gerten, Vera Heck, Timothy M. Lenton, and Hans Joachim Schellnhuber, "The Limits to Global-Warming Mitigation by Terrestrial Carbon Removal." *Earth's Future*, 5, No. 5 (May 2017): 463–474.
13. https://www.worldgbc.org/worldgreenbuildingweek, accessed 9 September 2020.
14. Ben Lamm, "Algae Might Be a Secret Weapon to Combatting Climate Change." Quartz, 30 September 2019. See also Richard Sayre, "Microalgae: The Potential for Carbon Capture." *BioScience*, 60, No. 9 (October 2010): 722–727. https://doi.org/10.1525/bio.2010.60.9.9.
15. ScienceDaily. "Clues to Trapping Carbon Dioxide in Rock: Calcium Carbonate Takes Multiple, Simultaneous Roads to Different Minerals". ScienceDaily, 4 September 2014.
16. S. Muryanto, A.P. Bayuseno, H. Ma'Mun, M. Usamah, and Jotho, "Calcium Carbonate Scale Formation in Pipes: Effect of Flow Rates, Temperature, and Malic Acid as Additives on the Mass and Morphology of the Scale." *Procedia Chemistry*, 9 (2014): 69–76.
17. N. Saifuddin, K. Aisswarya, Y.P. Juan, and P. Priatharsi, "Sequestration of High Carbon Dioxide Concentration for Induction of Lipids in Microalgae for Biodiesel Production." *Journal of Applied Sciences*, 15, No. 8 (January 2015): 1045–1058.

Index

Note: *Italic* page numbers refer to *figures*.

actor-network theory (ANT) 8, 10, 16–20, 22, 25, 27–28, 30–32
analysis 46, 47; needs and facts 42
Anderson, Jane 6
apocalypse 24
architectural education 1, 3–5; and real-world problems 5–6

Bakewell 105
Bandura 97
Banerjee, H. K. 97
Battleship Potemkin 27
Belfast 16, 19–22, 24–25, 27, 29–31
Birmingham 12, 73, 75, 76, 78, 81, 87, 88, 91
Birmingham Production Space (BPS): production space, field condition 79–80; proposal, developing 80; space for production, establishing 78–80
Black Lives Matter 7–8
bodies of water 18, 29–31
Bollington 105
Bosch, Hieronymus 25
Bradford 100
Bridges, A. 97
Bruner 97
BSoAD 75, 76, 78
Buchanan, Richard 96

Claxton, Ruth 76
climate change 3, 6, 8, 116, 118–120, 122, 123, 127, 129, 132, 134
co-designers 56, 66

Cole, Thomas 25
collaborative projects 12, 84, 95, 107
collection 42, 46
communication 22, 37, 53, 56, 58, 61, 64, 82
Conflict and Dialogue 59
Continuity in Architecture 94–112
"The Course of Empire" 25
COVID-19 2, 6, 7, 17, 32
cross-disciplinary/inter-disciplinary approaches 6
cumulus project 53–72
cyborg *24*

De Graff, E. 97
deindustrialisation 25
design-based learning 124, 125, 127
design-build education 57, 66
design-build studios 53, 55–57, 67
design education 1–4, 6, 8, 14, 36, 55, 62
Designing Resilience in Asia International Research Program (DRiA) 14, 116–120, 122–134; biological approach 129; chemical approach 129; direct air carbon systems 130; discourse and analysis 129–130; government and public agencies 133–134; green and blue CO_2 sequestration 129; real-world cases 133–134; statement and hypothesis 126–129; synthetic forest, city 132–133; synthetic forest strategies 129–130; synthetic leaves, systems 130–131; synthetic trees, buildings 131–132

138 Index

design process 5, 10, 28, 32, 36, 57, 59, 64, 66, 95, 96, 98, 124
design studios 5, 29, 46, 49, 53, 55, 56, 64, 82, 97, 116; collaboration in 56–57
design teams 17, 40, 43–46, 64
Design Thinking 36, 38, 40, 44, 46, 94, 96, 98–100, 109, 110
digital practices 7
digitisation 1
diversification 1
Dorst, Kees 40, 44
Duffy, T.M. 97

EAAE Charter 96
Eastside Projects 12, 75
EDIT studios 56, 67
educational organisation 6
educational practices 1
Eisenstein, Sergei 27
embedded collaboration 105–109
empathy/_mpathic design 36–52; Dr. Carter G. Woodson, life and legacy 43–44; empathic background, practice 37–38; empathic discovery 40–41, 44–45; empathic implementation 42–43, 48–49; experiential designing and making 41–42, 45–48; inspirations and influences 36–37; mapping 39, 43; methodology, mosaic 39–49; principles 38–39
empathy tour 41, 45
Engeström, Y. 57
exhibition 8, 10, 36–45, 47–49
external collaborator 6

"The Garden of Earthly Delights" 25

Haggard, Ben 119
Hart, Robert Lamb 39
Hauberg, Jorgen 125
Hayhurst, Nick 2
Heritage Schools Project 109
High Street/Future of the High Street 82, 95, 100, 102, 106, 107, 111
Historic High Street 95, 100, 106, 107
Hyde, Rory 2

idea 42
ideation (prototyping) 46, 47

identification 41, 45
IDEO 38, 39
interdisciplinary design teams 10, 40, 44
intervention 53–72; challenges 64–65; collaboration, design studios 56–57; design, youth participation 62–63; design-build studio 55; EDIT studio 56; implementing insights 62–63; participatory engagement, youth 59–62; project initiation 54–55; studio culture 63–64; studio framework 57–58
Ives, Courtney 104

Jefferson, Thomas 37

Keqin He 107
Koetter, Fred 99
Kraft-Todd, Gordon 40, 44

laboratories, exploration 3–4
Langdon, James 76
Lanzoni, Susan 39
Latour, Bruno 18
Lave 97
Localism Act 94, 105

Manchester School of Architecture 12, 94, 98, 99
Mang, Pamela 119
McLaren, Karla 37
The Mis-Education of the Negro 46

Neighbourhood Planning 107
Neimanis, Astrida 18, 30
Nencini, Peter 76
Northern Ireland 8, 16, 19, 22, 27

O'Donnell, Shelia 103
Oral History along the Lagan 25
Outram, John 105
outward-facing problem-based learning 95–98; problem-based learning 97; research-through-design 95–96; wicked problems 98

participatory learning 4–5
Patel, Abigail 2

place-focused project 111
Priest, Colin 6
Problem-Based Learning 4, 12, 94–112
production space 8, 12, 73–93
project-based learning 27
project partners 20, 21
project statement 127
Public CoLab 2019 16–35; educational approach 27–30

realization 47, 48
real-world problems 5–6
Reed, Bill 119
regenerative design 13, 119
Reiss, Helen 40, 44
Remember, Reveal, Construct 110–111
research by design approach 125
research-through-design 12, 94–96, 109; projects 95, 96, 100
"research-through-doing" methodology 4
resilience 116–136; active learning 124–125; amplifying urban design 123; climate challenge 118–119; co-learning 124–125; contemporary debates in urbanism 121–122; design-based learning 124–125; Designing Resilience in Asia International Research Program (DRiA) 117–118, 122, 125; designing with uncertainty 119–120; fast-changing, uncertain, and unpredictable environments 121–122; knowledge exchange and network collaboration 123; learning by doing 124; learning from experience 124; learning through design games 125–126; pedagogical objectives 120–123; regenerative design and development 119–120; research by design 125; teaching, research, practice and implementation 122–123; teaching urban design 117
Roberts, A. 97
Roberts, Bryony 103
Roberts Stone Studio 109

Rochdale 94–115; reimagined 99–105
Rochdale Borough Design Awards 109
Rohd, Michael. 59
Roma Interrotta 105
Rowe, Colin 99

Salama, Ashraf M. 4, 5
Savery, J.R. 97
scale bending 30
Schön, Donald 64
Schumacher, Thomas 99
Scruggs, Joe 50
Sert, Josep Lluis 116, 117
Shrewsbury 100
Silvetti, Jorge 99
Simon, Herbert A. 39
Singapore 13, 14, 117, 133, 134
"Spatial Design Education: New Directions for Pedagogy in Architecture and Beyond" 4
STEAM 1.5 89–90
STEAM design philosophy 73
STEAM education: in local context 75; political response 74–75
STEAMhouse 12, 74–76, 80–85, 87–91; building in city 81–82; creative clustering 84–85; housing STEAM thinking 80–85; insights from phase 1 87–89; management and technical team 90; public programme 85–87; public workspace 82–84; supporters, space for production 75–78
STEAM Inc. 85–87, 90
Strike 27
synthetic trees 14, 126, 131–133
"The Synthetic Tree & The Synthetic Forest" 14

Theater for Community 59
Till, Jeremy 16, 17
Timme, Elizabeth 98
Tracing Belfast's Water 21
transdisciplinary conceptualisation 29
Tuomey, John 98

urban design 3, 27, 55, 116–119, 122–124, 126
urban intervention *13*

urbanism 14, 116, 117, 120, 122, 123, 134

Verwijnen, Jan 80, 91
visitor experience 40, 43, 45, 46, 48, 49
Vyas, Dhaval 57, 61, 64, 66
Vygotsky 97

Wahl, Daniel Christian 119
water footprint, households *23*
water infrastructure 10, 18, 19, 21, 28, 31
water supply 18, 20, 22

wicked problems 3, 6, 12, 14, 30, 39, 94, 98, 99, 100, 109, 110, 112
"Wicked Problems in Design Thinking" 96
Wilmslow 105
Wiseman, Theresa 40, 44
Woodson, Carter G. 46
workshop 8, 16–35, 80, 81, 85; output, zine 21–27; structure 19–21; theoretical positioning 16–19

Zeiger, Mimi 110
Zhou, Yiting 104

For Product Safety Concerns and Information please contact our EU representative GPSR@taylorandfrancis.com
Taylor & Francis Verlag GmbH, Kaufingerstraße 24, 80331 München, Germany